FLY

IN THE

OINTMENT

PETER LANG
New York • Washington, D.C./Baltimore • Bern
Frankfurt am Main • Berlin • Brussels • Vienna • Oxford

PATRICIA RANDOLPH LEIGH

FLY

IN THE

OINTMENT

School Segregation and Desegregation
in the Ohio Valley

PETER LANG
New York • Washington, D.C./Baltimore • Bern
Frankfurt am Main • Berlin • Brussels • Vienna • Oxford

Library of Congress Cataloging-in-Publication Data

Leigh, Patricia Randolph.
Fly in the ointment: school segregation and desegregation
in the Ohio Valley / Patricia Randolph Leigh.
p. cm.
Includes bibliographical references.
1. Segregation in education—Ohio—History.
2. School integration—Ohio—History. I. Title.
LC212.522.O3L45   379.2'63'09771—dc22   2004015778
ISBN 0-8204-6712-X

Bibliographic information published by **Die Deutsche Bibliothek**.
Die Deutsche Bibliothek lists this publication in the "Deutsche
Nationalbibliografie"; detailed bibliographic data is available
on the Internet at http://dnb.ddb.de/.

Cover design by Joni Holst

The paper in this book meets the guidelines for permanence and durability
of the Committee on Production Guidelines for Book Longevity
of the Council of Library Resources.

© 2005 Peter Lang Publishing, Inc., New York
275 Seventh Avenue, 28th Floor, New York, NY 10001
www.peterlangusa.com

Printed in the United States of America

To the People of Lincoln Heights
Past, Present, and Future

Contents

Acknowledgments

I would like to express my gratitude to several people who helped me throughout this process. Among the friends and colleagues to whom I am grateful are Ann D. Thompson and Jackie M. Blount who supported the initial conception of this book during my doctoral studies. I would also like to thank Willis Holloway, Eddie L. Starr, Ernest Ector, Florence Snell, and Flora Alexander for sharing their time, support, and their life experiences which are contained in this work.

I am also grateful to the Ford Foundation for a postdoctoral fellowship award administered by the National Research Council, which enabled me to conduct much of the research contained in this book.

Grateful acknowledgment is hereby made to copyright holders for permission to use the following copyrighted material:

Leigh, Patricia R. (1997). "Segregation by Gerrymander: The Creation of the Lincoln Heights (Ohio) School District," *Journal of Negro Education,* vol. 66, nos. 2, pp. 121-136.
Permission is granted to reprint the article noted above for use.

Leigh, Patricia R. (2003). "Interest Convergence and Desegregation in the Ohio Valley," *Journal of Negro Education,* vol. 72, nos. 3, pp. 269-296. Permission is granted to reprint the article noted above for use.

Introduction

Fly in the Ointment chronicles the of history two school districts located in the upper Mill Creek (Ohio) Valley of the Greater Cincinnati Metropolitan area. The creation of the Black Lincoln Heights School District (LHSD) and the predominately White Princeton School District (PSD) is a history of segregation, while the merger of these two districts, close to twenty years after their formation, tells a unique story of desegregation.

In the Shadow of *Brown*

While this story, as many others, takes place in the context of the Supreme Court ruling of *Brown v. Board of Education, Topeka, KS* of 1954, it is unique in several ways. First, as the story unfolds in chapter 2, "Segregation by Gerrymander: The Creation of the Lincoln Heights (Ohio) School District," it unveils a history of racial and economic discrimination that culminated in the creation of an all-Black school district. This occurred in the early 1950s just as segregation cases were being brought forth by the NAACP Legal Defense Fund in lower courts across the country, cases that would later be consolidated and heard in the highest court of the land. (see Kluger, 1977) In 1952, the Supreme Court agreed to hear the consolidated school segregation cases from South Carolina, Virginia, Delaware, Kansas, and the District of Columbia. So while these NAACP lawyers were fighting legalized segregation that had been in existence for decades, particularly in the South, these northern communities in the Greater Cincinnati Metropolitan area were moving in the opposite direction. By 1954 when the *Brown* decision was rendered, the Hamilton (Ohio) County Board of Education had submitted a consolidation plan that would include seven White districts surrounding but not including Lincoln Heights. De facto segregation in this Ohio valley was being strengthened just as national attention was given to dismantling segregation de jure.

The Princeton School District was officially formed in 1955 and ultimately included eight local districts; an additional predominately White district was added after the initial seven-district consolidation plan. The histories of these communities and districts are outlined in chapters 3 and 4. Interestingly, *Brown II* was also rendered in 1955, which ordered the desegregation of schools "with all deliberate speed." In spite of this admonition, both the new all-Black Lincoln Heights High School and the new Princeton High School, which would help serve the recently formed predominately White district, opened their doors in the 1958–59 academic year. This situation was not successfully challenged until the late 1960s, and this account is outlined in chapter 6.

Fly in the Ointment also underscores the nuances of race and class as it reveals how citizens in the new district struggled with the acceptance of those that threatened their homogeneity. However, race trumped socioeconomic class concerning the issue of exclusion because the economically poor but White Stewart district was included whereas the economically poor and Black Lincoln Heights district was not.

The desegregation and merging of these two northern districts is also unique in that it did not come about as a direct result of court actions as did other Ohio districts. The Lincoln Heights and Princeton merger took place well before the Sixth District Court's ruling of *Penick v. Columbus Board of Education* in 1977, which declared that "the defendants were guilty of intentionally creating and maintaining illegally segregated school systems." (Jacobs, 1998, p. 4) The *Penick* ruling was the impetus for desegregating public schools in Columbus, Ohio. During this same period, the NAACP was fighting to desegregate Dayton, Ohio public schools. This battle began with *Brinkman v. Gilligan* (1973), and culminated with *Brinkman v. Gilligan* (1978) in the Court of Appeals of the Sixth Circuit. Judge Phillips wrote, "that to the time of Brown I, defendants intentionally operated a dual system and never fulfilled their affirmative duty to eliminate…segregation." (as cited in Watras, 1997, p. 197) In 1979, the Supreme Court upheld the decision of the court of appeals.

The Lincoln Heights and Princeton merger also occurred three years before the Supreme Court ruling in *Keyes v. Denver School District* (1973) and one year before the Court's ruling in *Swann v. Charlotte-Mecklenburg Board of Education* (1971). On the other hand, *Keyes* and *Swann* heavily influenced both the Dayton and Columbus cases. (Jacobs, 1998; Watras, 1997) *Keyes* is important in that it was "the first ruling on school segregation in the North and West, where there were no explicit statutes requiring segregation." (Orfield, Eaton & The Harvard Project on School Desegregation, 1996, p. xxii) Orfield et al. go on to state, "Under *Keyes*, school districts were responsible for policies that resulted in racial segregation in the school system, including constructing schools in racially isolated neighborhoods and gerrymandering attendance zones." (p. xxii) Jacobs (1998) concurs in stating: "By rendering the distinction between de facto and de jure school segregation virtually irrelevant, *Keyes* threw open the door to desegregation in northern and western cities." (p. 45)

Swann was an important judicial ruling that approved busing as a remedy in cases where segregated districts were results of residential segregation. "Thus while Swann proclaimed bussing a permissible remedial tool," Jacobs (1998) explains, "the Court stopped short of applying the decision to northern segregation. Nevertheless, for cities outside of the South, the handwriting was on the wall." (p. 33)

These landmark decisions that occurred before, during, and after the segregation and desegregation of the Lincoln Heights and Princeton districts give a sense of the racial and political climate that was in place. Furthermore, perhaps this climate created handwritings on the wall even before *Penick, Keyes,* and *Swann.* Ultimately, as pointed out in chapter 6, the threat of legal action was the leverage used to accelerate talks of annexation and the eventual merger of the Lincoln Heights and Princeton districts.

Viewing Desegregation through a Critical Race Theory "Lens"

In 1970, the Princeton School District agreed to accept 1,900 Black students from the neighboring, economically depressed community of Lincoln Heights, Ohio. Understanding the complex and interlocking political, social, economic, and racial factors that lead to segregation, desegregation, and, more recently, resegregation is often difficult. Critical Race Theory (CRT), a paradigm originating out of the legal field, has potential for "making sense" of the actions of the major players in these racial segregation/integration scenarios. Though this paradigm has its roots in the legal field, it is a philosophical lens that allows one to bring into focus issues of race and class dominance in the general society as well as in specific institutions such as those within the U.S. education system. CRT can be used to clarify not only the rules of law and the rulings of American courts, such as found in school segregation cases, but can also bring insight to the analysis of rules that govern society and communities concerning these issues.

While racial segregation and desegregation of schools and educational systems are considered directly related to the presence or lack of equal opportunities for American children, their histories have not been explored from a theoretical framework. In the specific historical accounts of the de-segregation and merger of the Princeton (PSD) and Lincoln Heights (LHSD) school districts, this is especially true. While there were many newspaper accounts, both current and reflective, none attempted to report the events through a particular philosophical or theoretical lens. Lucas (1971, 1976), the superintendent of PDS during the merger, wrote concerning the successful outcome with little reference to and no in-depth analysis of the factors that led to the segregation of Lincoln Heights or its merger with Princeton. The 1971 title, "Princeton's Investment in Children Provides New Opportunities for All," hints heavily of the benevolence of the Princeton district in accept-ing the neighboring Black children. Lucas talks about the revocation of the Lincoln Heights charter and the positive resolution of the Princeton board of education after the Ohio State board of education transferred the Lincoln Heights students. There is no mention of the Lincoln Heights board's in-volvement in initiating the merger and little emphasis placed on the threat-ened legal action. On the other hand, Lucas credits much of the success of the merger to the Princeton school board's commitment to integration and details many of the phase-in programs and school and community activities he and the board initiated and implemented to assure a smooth transfer.

Similarly, Luke (1981a, 1981b, 1982) wrote a series of historical ac-counts of the emergence and growth of the Princeton School district, but they too lack philosophical or theoretical analysis and also omit facts concerning the involvement of the Lincoln Heights community or school board in the LHSD/PSD merger. In fact, one may perceive from the above mentioned accounts that the decision to accept the Black students into the predominately White school system was driven by the good-hearted will of the White com-munity members and by their commitment to equality of opportunity. Such motivation is contrary to what history reveals about the prevailing attitudes that led to the isolation of these same students and in the creation of the seg-regated Lincoln Heights (Ohio) School District of the 1950s. (Taylor, 1993; see also chapter 2) In fact, attitudes were quite opposite to those expressed by Lucas and others a mere 20 years later and to the pervasiveness of racism proposed by Critical Race theorists.

In addressing the problem of the lack of theorizing race when examining the issues of educational inequalities in the United States, Ladson-Billings and Tate (1995) note:

> By arguing that race remains untheorized, we are not suggesting that other scholars
> have not looked carefully at race as a powerful tool for explaining social inequity,
> but that the intellectual salience of this theorizing has not been systematically em-
> ployed in the analysis of educational inequality. (p. 50)

These authors show, using Critical Race Theory as an analytical tool, the connection between race, property, and education. This connection is especially important to the current research in that the creation of school districts is directly related to property rights, and race-based segregation and desegregation in American schools impacts the level of equality between districts. Critical Race theorist Cheryl Harris (1995) explores the issue of property rights as related to race and maintains that, in the U.S., race "whiteness" is an actual property right. Central to the Harris concept of "whiteness as property" is the "absolute right to exclude." Harris suggests, "The possessors of whiteness were granted the legal right to exclude others from the privileges inhering in whiteness; whiteness became an exclusive club whose membership was closely and grudgingly guarded." (p. 283) The creation and segregation of the Lincoln Heights city properties and the school district boundaries based upon racial discrimination and gerrymandering (see Taylor, 1979 and chapter 2) are glaring examples of the "absolute right to exclude" at work.

Critical Race Theory maintains that racism is endemic and pervasive in American society to the extent that all but the most blatant, egregious racist behaviors and attitudes are considered normal:

> [R]acism is normal, not aberrant, in American society. Because racism is an in-
> grained feature of our landscape, it looks ordinary and natural to persons in the cul-
> ture. Formal equal opportunity—rules and laws that insist on treating blacks and
> whites (for example) alike—can thus remedy only the more extreme and shocking
> sorts of injustice, the ones that do stand out. Formal equality can do little about the
> business-as-usual forms of racism that people of color confront every day and that
> account for much misery, alienation, and despair. (Delgado, 1995, p. xiv)

In using CRT to guide their research, Solorzano, Ceja, and Yosso (2000) summarize the literature concerning the meaning of racism and delineate three points common to the accepted definitions:

> (1) one group believes itself to be superior

(2) the group that believes itself to be superior has the power to carry out the racist behavior, and

(3) racism affects multiple racial and ethnic groups. (p. 61)

This pervasive racism can take the form of unconscious racism as described by Lawrence (1995). He purports that practically all people having been exposed and immersed in American society have racist attitudes. Because racism has recently become socially unacceptable, Lawrence contends that most citizens will not acknowledge these attitudes nor allow them to rise from the unconscious to the conscious level.

The concept of interest convergence, another important tenet that arises out of CRT, can explain why those who are generally opposed to policies supporting racial equality would suddenly concede and appear, at least on the surface, committed to the highly touted American concept of equality of opportunity for all:

> Developed by Derrick Bell, this idea holds that white elites will tolerate or encourage racial advances for blacks only when they also promote white self-interest. Other Criticalists question whether civil rights law is designed to benefit blacks, and even suggest that it is really a homeostatic mechanism that ensures that racial progress occurs at just the right pace: change that is too rapid would be unsettling to society at large; change that is too slow could prove destabilizing. Many question whether white judges are likely to propel racial change, raising the possibility that nonjudicial avenues may prove more promising. A number of writers employ Critical tools to address such classic civil rights issues as federal law, remedies for racist speech and hate-motivated crime, and women's reproductive liberty. (Delgado, 1995, p. xiv)

Interest convergence adherents contend that White Americans will support racial equality only when such policies advance their own interests or at least do not seriously disrupt the status quo. Bell, for example, explains that while many liberal Whites support the *Brown v Board of Education* decision in theory, these same individuals would hinder its true implementation or application in practice when such an implementation failed to validate or, more importantly, threatens to undermine their dominant status. (Bell, 1980, 1987, 1992) Bell (1980) writes:

> [T]his principle of "interest convergence" provides: *The interest of blacks in achieving racial equality will be accommodated only when it converges with the interests of whites; however, the fourteenth amendment, standing alone, will not authorize a*

judicial remedy providing effective racial equality for blacks where the remedy sought threatens the superior societal status of middle- and upper-class whites. (Original emphasis; p. 95)

Thus interest convergence, according to Bell, explains why the nine Supreme Court justices unanimously outlawed state-mandated segregation and thereby cleaned up America's image to look less like that of the defeated Nazi Germany. Interest convergence also explains why subsequent Supreme Court rulings have served to dismantle desegregation, as described by Orfield, Eaton and The Harvard Project on School Desegregation (1996), or why court rulings make irrelevant the *Brown* decision when advancing racial equality does not directly serve the dominant racial/ethnic group and would diminish the racial privileges they have historically enjoyed.

The name *Fly in the Ointment* seems appropriate for this body of work for the following reasons. The racism that abounded in Cincinnati during the early 1900s gave rise to the Black community of Lincoln Heights. This community, dense with unwanted African Americans, sat on rich industrial properties and was located in the midst of surrounding wealthy White communities. From the White racist perspective, Lincoln Heights not only visually resembled a "fly in the ointment" but also represented the fly that threatened to ruin plans for building and maintaining a "pure and uncontaminated" consolidated school district while, at the same time, capturing all the rich industrial land.

Fly in the Ointment uses various methodologies to provide an accurate account from various perspectives of school segregation and desegregation in a specific region of the country. This body of work includes "fictional" storytelling—an approach supported by alternative research methodologies, particularly Critical Race Theory. This storytelling, presented in chapter 1, is combined in this book with chapters containing historical data from primary and secondary sources and interview data presented using qualitative analysis and methodology. The purpose of utilizing this unique combination of approaches is to document an important historical story yet to be told and, more importantly, to tell a complete story that includes all important voices. For this reason, the more traditional historical research methodology is encompassed by the alternative narrative approaches.

Analyzing the Lincoln Heights and Princeton Merger

I bring to this research the bias of Critical Race Theory (CRT) and interpret the historical events surrounding the school districts under study through the CRT perspective. The CRT tenet that proposes the pervasiveness of racism in American society was demonstrated in the machinations that led to racial segregation of communities and school districts in the Ohio Mill Creek Valley. To adequately examine the motivations for and implications of desegregation of these specific school districts, one needs to look first at the factors that led to segregation.

Removing Blacks from the rich industrial Valley View subdivision, as described in chapter 3, is disturbingly similar to other more massive and egregious federally sponsored removals of ethnic minorities when such actions had economic benefits for the dominant White majority. Critical Race theorists contend that American government and society are based on property rights rather than human or individual rights, and this emphasis fosters and rationalizes injustices such as those experienced by Native Americans, Japanese Americans, and the residents of the Valley View subdivision in Ohio. (Bell, 1995; Harris, 1995) Ladson-Billings and Tate (1995) concur:

> The grand narrative of U.S. history is replete with tensions and struggles over property—in its various forms. From the removal of Indians (and later Japanese Americans) from the land, to military conquest of the Mexicans, to the construction of Africans as property, the ability to define, possess, and own property has been a central feature of power in America....However, the contradiction of a reified symbolic individual juxtaposed [to] the reality of "real estate" means that emphasis on the centrality of property can be disguised. Thus, we talk about the importance of the individual, individual rights, and civil rights while social benefits accrue largely to property owners. (p. 53)

According to the citizens of Lincoln Heights, who had once inhabited the very land on which the General Electric plant was erected, justice was denied when this valuable property was eliminated from their incorporation or annexation petitions and awarded to their White wealthy neighbors. Critical Race Theory explains that justice did not prevail in these instances because of the lack of interest convergence. The interests of the Black citizens of Lincoln Heights needed to converge or intersect with those of the dominant White power structures. What, in fact, occurred was the opposite; the interests of the African American communities in this region were at odds with those in power. It did not benefit the government or the Defense Corporation for Lincoln Heights to incorporate the land on which the Wright Aeronautical Plant was built. To avoid the responsibility of supporting this populace community with taxes, the Defense Corporation used its influence to see that an incorporation including these properties did not happen. In later years, Lincoln Heights again failed in its efforts to secure the land through annexation. The neighboring community of Evandale, wealthy and sparsely populated by comparison, succeeded in acquiring this property on which the General Electric Plant would be built.

Critical Race Theory would also locate race at the center of the conflict. Not only was Lincoln Heights heavily populated, it was populated by African Americans. These Black subdivisions that later formed a village did not come into being as a result of benign, colorblind policies but were the direct outcomes of racist attitudes reflected in formal and informal laws. Critical Race Theory purports that racism is an ingrained feature of the American fabric and colors every aspect of life in this society, specifically for African Americans and other minorities. Therefore, one can speculate that had the inhabitants of the original Valley View subdivision been White, the outcome of the incorporation efforts may have been considerably different. White racism portrays African Americans as inferior and views this inherent inferiority as justification for denying access to opportunities. Lincoln Heights residents were segregated as a result of racist attitudes and policies, and it is reasonable to conclude that decisions concerning which communities should and would benefit from the incorporation of the rich industrial properties were also influenced or determined by these same racist beliefs. As Bell (1995) contends:

> A major function of racial discrimination is to...deny us access to benefits and opportunities that would otherwise be available, and to blame all the manifestations of exclusion-bred despair on the asserted inferiority of the victims. (p. 75)

In these instances, racism and the lack of interest convergence prevented a just and equitable outcome for the Black residents in the Ohio valley.

The history of the emergence of the incorporated villages, unincorporated towns, and the individual school districts that would later become part of the new Princeton district is a history of exclusion. (see chapters 3 and 4) This story validates Harris's (1995) premise that there are property rights in Whiteness. White people who settled in the communities in the Ohio Valley exercised those rights vigorously by maintaining racially homogeneous towns and schools. In the event that small numbers of Black Americans were somehow able to settle within the borders of these villages or towns, racially separate schools were maintained. However, the masses of African Americans who found themselves in this valley were contained in the Black subdivisions that later became the village/city of Lincoln Heights. "The right to exclude," an important property right in Whiteness, was a common practice in the nation as a whole and in the history of the Ohio Valley in particular. The right to keep trespassers or "others" out is the right of any property owner. Those who possessed "Whiteness" took this right to heart when dealing with the African American "others" who inhabited this region. The actions of Woodlawn and the board of education described in chapter 2 set the stage for Lincoln Heights' isolation and subsequent exclusion from future district consolidations. Again Critical Race Theory contends that the endemic nature of racism in American society fosters attitudes, policies, and laws that easily justify Lincoln Heights' treatment by Woodlawn and the county board. Tate (1996) asserts, "Both educational research and law have often characterized 'raced' people as intellectually inferior and raised doubts about the benefit of equitable social investment in education and other social services." (p. 202)

It was also necessary to thoroughly examine the economic inequities in the development of the communities involved in order to adequately understand the educational inequities fostered during 20 years of segregation. Comparing the per-pupil valuations of the schools in the districts under study, as outlined in chapter 5, clearly shows that inequities existed throughout this time period. These gross inequities continued, with no significant external intervention efforts, during the years that Lincoln Heights School District existed and indicates that the blatant racism that motivated the gerrymandering had taken on a face of normalcy. Racial justice could have easily been accomplished at any time, either by including Lincoln Heights in the initial consolidation of districts to form the Princeton School District or at any time hence. From a Critical Race perspective, knowledge of this racism calls into question the notion that desegregation in this instance was truly the result of predominately White communities "rescuing" a depressed, predominantly Black school district.

The role played by interest convergence in the history of the segregation and desegregation of the Lincoln Heights and Princeton school districts seems all too obvious. Social justice, in this case access to equal educational opportunities, was afforded the Black children of the Lincoln Heights community only when doing so benefited the neighboring White communities and districts. The threat of legal suit and the accompanying negative publicity was a significant factor in causing the interests of Whites to converge with the interests of Blacks. Once the decision was made to absorb Lincoln Heights into the Princeton School District, media reports still managed to attribute to the White participants superior, benevolent qualities, thus somewhat maintaining the status quo in terms of racial relationships. If they were depending upon newspaper accounts at the time of the revocation of the Lincoln Heights charter and the subsequent merger with the Princeton district, most Cincinnatians would have been unaware of the active struggle in which the Black participants engaged. Interest convergence demands that the status quo not be severely altered as a result of granting social justice. Giving 1,900 Black students access to White schools and educational resources while maintaining the stereotypic images of White benevolent patriarchy and Black childlike passivity (even after decades of struggle) is a brilliant example of this important aspect of interest convergence.

Although Critical Race Theory purports the endemic nature of racism in American society and the near impossibility of acquiring justice without the presence of interest convergence, it nevertheless underscores the importance for the oppressed to struggle against and resist their oppression. This research also gives voice to the perspectives of the Black educators who lived and worked through the segregation and desegregation of schools in this region of Ohio. Their voiced experiences, found in chapters 7 and 8, lend power and authenticity to the words found in other primary or secondary sources such as board minutes, newspaper articles, and reports. At the same time, these Black administrators and teachers provide a kind of triangulation and validation of some data while rendering a different interpretation of other data. Moreover, they provide windows into the board meetings, classrooms, and the communities where resistance often took place. Bell (1992), when outlining a theory of racial realism, contends that past success or failure should not determine whether one should resist when faced with injustices. According to Bell:

> [W]e believe in fulfillment—some might call it salvation—through struggle. We reject any philosophy that insists on measuring life's success on the achieving of specific goals—overlooking the process of living. More affirmatively and as a matter of

faith, we believe that, despite the lack of linear progress, there is satisfaction in the struggle itself. (p. 98)

The leaders and citizens of Lincoln Heights demonstrated this type of resistance as they continued to seek justice for their community despite a history of racial discrimination and many years of failed attempts.

PART I

Myths and Tales

CHAPTER 1

The Tale of the Benevolent White School District

This tale deconstructs the notion of the benevolence that is often attributed to the dominant White patriarchy—a patriarchy that grants social justice or rescues the dominated from their demise. Moreover, this tale gives voice to the experiences, emotions, attitudes, politics, and passions of the African Americans in a segregated population that is surrounded by yet isolated from wealthy White communities. Though the tale itself is fictional, the events are based on fact, and the characters are representative of individuals with whom I interacted or had knowledge of. The characters that lived and struggled in Liberty Heights, as described in this tale, mirror real inhabitants of Lincoln Heights and their reaction to the actual events that occurred in the Ohio valley. I grew up in Lincoln Heights and was privy to the conversations and stories surrounding the issues outlined in the subsequent chapters, and I was aware of the attitudes of family members and other community members concerning these issues. The names of the communities, people, newspapers, etc. have been changed, yet all existed. The tale is fictional and the characters are representative in that, in some cases, one character may voice the opinions and attitudes of several people. This tale allows for the engagement of those whose perspectives are not found in historical documents and are inaccessible by interview. Storytelling is an essential ingredient in the philosophy that undergirds *Fly in the Ointment* and is used extensively by Critical Race theorists such as Derrick Bell (1987,1992).

The Randles

On February 3, 1970, the headline in the *Mill Creek Star* read "Orphan Black Students Adopted by Whites." Seventy-two-year-old Minerva Jane Randle examined the article carefully. "Nervie," as her friends called her, had been a resident of the "depressed predominately black" community of Liberty Heights since her family migrated from the South in 1923. This particular article captured her interest because it described the fate of the "orphan" students of the Liberty Heights community and school district.

"Ain't that a blip," Nervie responded aloud to herself, or perhaps to her cat, Blackie, after reading a statement attributed to the State Superintendent of Public Instruction.

> The transfer would be the first time anywhere in the country that a depressed, predominately black school district was rescued by neighboring affluent, predominately white communities.

The article told of the neighboring Price Valley school district's agreement to absorb the Liberty Heights School District and thereby transfer close to 1,800 Black students into its system. None of this was shocking news to Mrs. Randle. She spent many evenings rocking and dipping snuff on the porch with her good friend and neighbor, Abigail Hicks, and talking about the recent closings of Liberty Heights schools and all the rumors concerning the future of these students. Both Bee, as Abigail was called, and Nervie had seen Liberty Heights struggle and grow from a Black settlement of shanty houses to a village and finally to a self-sufficient city. Through the years they sat and rocked night after night on the same porch and discussed the current or impending trials and tribulations of the Liberty Heights community—many of which were brought on by these same white communities that now make up the Price Valley district.

"Rescued, huh?"

Blackie, who was curled up at the opposite end of the divan, slowly got up, dropped to the floor and walked out of the room with a definite air of indifference. Blackie was generally interested in gossip, rumors, and actual events that affected the community, but for some unknown reason he headed for the solitude of the back bedroom windowsill. Nervie barely noticed his departure as she focused on the particulars of this "rescue" mission. First of all, these depressed Liberty Heights residents would have to pay higher school taxes, and second, "some 14 acres valued at $110,000" in the Liberty Heights municipality also would be transferred to Price Valley. The third fact in this rescue mission that struck Mrs. Randle as odd (yet somehow predictable) was the fact that the valuable ammunitions plant property would be transferred from Lowlands—a community neither in the Liberty nor Price Valley school districts—to the Price Valley School District for tax purposes.

"Uh-uh-uh," Nervie muttered. She thought it odd (yet again predictable) that the article made no mention of how the actions of many of "neighboring, affluent, predominately white communities" were complicent in creating Liberty Heights' desperate situation from which they now needed to be rescued. It made no mention of the Liberty Heights leaders and residents who had fought for the betterment of their community in general and of their school system in particular. It made no mention of the conflicting views within the Liberty Heights community concerning what was best for the educational future of its children. It made no mention of the groups of Liberty Heights leaders and citizen committees that negotiated, cajoled, pleaded, and threatened its "benevolent" neighbors and those in authority over them in order to set this merger in motion.

"Lord, Lord, Lord," was all she could say aloud, but she remembered it all as images from the past flashed through her mind in rapid-fire fashion much like the compilation of video clips of past events often seen on television on or around every New Year.

Images…images…images

a tenement dwelling…

a plot of land…

children…

grandchildren…

schools built…

schools opened…

schools closed…

schools consolidated…

Fred and Minerva Randle came to the Ohio valley from Georgia in 1923 with eight of the ten children they would raise—the last two children were born north of the Mason-Dixon line. Neighbors from their southern homestead had settled in this region, and with their help the Randles were able to secure a living space in the crowded industrial center.

The Randles were used to the dirt poverty of the South, barely scratching out a living by sharecropping. But the urban poverty was another matter. They had never before felt crowded when they were outside in the open air—now they did. And there were new dangers to contend with. At the old homestead, if the children were not old enough to help in the house or field, they

were relatively free to roam and play around and in the yard or tag along behind Minerva as she drew water from the well, washed clothes from a tin tub,
and hung them on a line, tree, or bush. Now washing was a real challenge,
and clothesline space was limited to that shared by the other tenement dwell-
ers on the roof of the building. The safest place for the young children was in
the confines of the small apartment. Outside those walls were filth and industrial waste, crime, and the dangers of people, machines, and animals on the
outside road that came right up to the door of the tenement building. There
was no yard or field to act as buffer between the building and the outside
world. In fact, the youngest child, Mabel, two years old at the time, found
herself on the ground, face down under a horse-drawn buggy—miraculously
staying clear of the wheels of the carriage and the feet of the horse—after
darting from the door of the tenement into the road one morning when her
mother's back was turned.

So although poverty was nothing new to the Randles, they were disap-
pointed that their new urban life did not more closely approximate their rural
life. They had migrated North with so many others in search of work and a
better life after the demise of many farms, both small and large, had made it
virtually impossible for the poorest of the poor to survive. Like the other
Black families that had moved into the Ohio River basin area of this industrial city, the Randles sought work in the burgeoning industries and held on
to their belief that they could carve out a life for their family in this urban
center.

Minerva heard about the Black subdivision from her neighbor and friend,
Bee, who was living in the same tenement with her husband Vernon and
their child. It was rumored soon after their arrival in 1923 that lots were being sold to Blacks in an industrial subdivision about 15 miles north of the
river basin area. The rumors turned out to be true, and Bee and her family
were one of the first to escape the crowded tenement. Over a three-year period Minerva managed to visit the Hickses and see that this new community
afforded a rural-like lifestyle. Though early on most of the structures were
mere shanties, the lack of zoning or building codes allowed the raising of
chickens, pigs, and other animals right in the front or back yards. It was also
possible to make a small garden, and the children could play in the yards or
even in the roads without the risk that they faced in the downtown basin.

In 1926 Fred, Minerva, and their children moved into this northern industrial subdivision. They rented a house that had been vacated by a more

"well-to-do" family that had moved on to a better home a few roads over. Fred had secured a job at a fertilizer plant nearby, and Minerva washed, cleaned, and cooked for a family in a neighboring all-White community and returned home to do the same for her family.

In the end, Fred and Minerva had ten children—five girls and five boys. As the children grew older they were able to contribute to the upkeep of the household, but for the most part, this was a challenge that both Fred and Minerva took squarely on their shoulders. Though Fred would often complain to the children, "You keep my nose to the grindstone," he was a faithful worker and managed to handle most of their living expenses. Minerva sewed, cooked, gardened, raised chickens, made lye soap, and generally pinched pennies in order to save enough money to purchase a lot a few doors down from her friend Bee on Adams Street—one street over from their Jackson Street house.

The Lanes

"Are you up yet?" Minerva inquired of her sleepy-eyed daughter as the latter opened the door of her home on Chester Road.

"Come on in, Mama."

It was six-o'-clock on the morning of a mild spring day in 1955. It was nothing for Minerva to arise early, complete her morning chores, put on a clean apron, and set out to walk the mile to visit her daughter's family. Of course no one in the Lane family was awake so early on this Saturday morning, but Mabel would not dream of indicating that her mother's visit was anything but welcome. And indeed it was welcome. If Mabel's "sleep-in-late" children heard Grandma's voice they would stumble into the kitchen to visit and listen to her tales.

"Grandma tell the story about Herchel Muggins," Pat asked that morning.

"Oh, child, that Herchel was a character. It was during the War when meat was scarce and rationed out. Ole Herchel and a bunch of his cronies went over in Woodlane and stole Mr. Flanigan's cow and hiked it back to Liberty Heights. Now it was raining that day, and they had sense enough to know that the cow would leave tracks, especially in our muddy streets, so those jokers put two pair of shoes on the cow's four feet and marched it straight home. I tell you, that was a funny sight to behold. Lord knows that I don't uphold no thieving, but that was sure a funny sight."

Tears of laughter were running down Pat's face. Grandma sure could tell a good tale.

Of the Randles' ten children, the Lanes were mostly affected by Liberty Heights' school situation in the 1950s, for the other sons and daughters had either moved from the area or did not have school-age children themselves. Thomas Lane, Jr., and Mabel Randle Lane had three—Tom III, Kassy, and Pat. To hear Pat tell it, she was the most affected.

On a more serious note, Pat asked, "Grandma, what does Mr. Hicks think about the new high school being built here?" Pat knew that he had been on the council when Liberty Heights was struggling for incorporation. She also knew that Vernon Hicks had been on the Liberty Heights first council and had been against the incorporation of the village. The Hickses, and the Randles for that matter, believed that incorporation might cause them to lose their property because of higher taxes and stricter building codes and zones. Grandma had told Pat that White folks at the fertilizer plant where Papa Randle worked had said as much. When Liberty Heights was incorporated and, according to most of the residents, cheated out of the fertilizer plant that should have afforded the community a reasonable tax base, those who were against incorporation could only say "I told you so." Though they did not lose their property because of higher taxes nor were they immediately required to relinquish the livestock in their front and back yards, the loss of the fertilizer plant verified their belief that the White bankers, businessmen, and whoever else was involved could not be trusted. It was all a trick to make these poor property owners even more vulnerable than before. Pat knew that Mr. Hicks and Papa Randle had agreed on just about everything, whether it was political, social, or spiritual. Though Fred Randle had been dead going on ten years, Pat knew that if she secured Vernon Hicks's opinion, she would likely know how Papa Randle would have felt about the new school.

"We were just talking about that this morning. Well, we are in a fix now. Mr. Hicks says he would just as soon have our school now since Woodlane and all the rest of the White folks around us have made it perfectly clear that they don't want our children in their schools. He said he don't want any of his grandchildren mistreated because they are not wanted."

Pat said, "But Daddy said that we don't have enough money to build a school much less run one. He said we won't have enough books or teachers. I don't want to go to a school with no books or teachers."

"Well, child, I don't know about all of that. But I am sure Vernon would say we are in this mess because we insisted on incorporation and set ourselves up to be cheated. Just yesterday evening he said if we had that fertilizer plant, maybe we would have enough money—he said we should have known all along that the White man was not going to let that happen."

Pat was troubled about the whole situation. She knew that Papa Lane, Thomas Lane, Sr., had also been on the council during the incorporation struggle and had fought long and hard for the independence of Liberty Heights. After he died, her father, Thomas, Jr., joined the ranks of those seeking the betterment of Liberty Heights through incorporation. He also fought for inclusion in the recently consolidated Price Valley School district, believing that it would provide Pat and her siblings a good education. In fact, her father had a hard time forgiving those who tried to impede incorporation, believing that they were purposely standing in the way of progress and even suspected that they were being used by Whites to delay the process. He told Pat on numerous occasions that if anti-incorporation groups had not delayed the process, Liberty Heights may well have secured the fertilizer plant and other industrial properties that were requested. He would not have agreed with Vernon Hicks that the pro-incorporation groups had set the community up to be cheated. Quite the opposite. But now that Woodlane and Oddale had all the good properties within their boundaries, leaving the Liberty Heights village and school district without adequate funds to support itself, Lane felt that the best educational solution was to annex to a neighboring district rather than build a new high school. He also had a tough time forgiving those who opposed the merger of the Liberty Heights school district with the recently consolidated Price Valley District. He just couldn't understand why some of his neighbors would stand in the way of what was obviously best for the Liberty Heights children. Pat knew he was fairly passionate about this issue, so she never would have inquired about Mr. Hicks's opinion if her father had not been fast asleep that early Saturday morning.

But to Minerva's last comment, Pat merely responded, "I see." She was not about to disrespect Grandpa Randle or Mr. Hicks, but she agreed with her father and therefore also agreed with her Grandfather Lane.

The Lanes had migrated from Georgia also but not from dirt poverty by any means. There seemed to be nothing that Pat's father enjoyed more than talking about the good ole days and growing up in Georgia with his brother and two sisters. Papa Lane had inherited land passed down through the years from a child born to a slave owner and slave. He had sharecroppers on the land and an abundance of fruit orchards, vegetable gardens, hayfields, chickens, cows, and game for hunting. The year that Lane, Sr., failed to diversify his crops and planted all cotton was the year that the boll weevils stripped his land and left him bankrupt. He moved first to Pennsylvania seeking work in the steel mills, leaving his family in Georgia for two years. After securing enough funds, he moved to Liberty Heights to work for a homebuilder in the area and sent for his family in 1926 when Thomas, Jr., was 12 years old.

Pat's father was involved in several business enterprises, but his main occupation during her early school years was building houses in Liberty Heights. These were wonderful homes, well known for their smooth solid plastered walls and finished hardwood floors. If the city did not provide a street or sidewalk to face his newly built string of bungalows, then Thomas, Jr., would simply pour them himself. As a result of his passion for houses, the Lanes moved more than most—probably more than any family in the history of Liberty Heights. The moving stopped when her mother grew weary of packing and refused to budge again. At any rate, one of their moves took the family quite a distance from the public school that Pat was attending, so she began third grade at St. Althea's Episcopal School in the "upper sub" of Liberty Heights. From that point, the family lived within comfortable walking distance of this elementary school.

In the Lane household, if the children wanted money for some purchase they simply needed to say, "it's for school." That was a standing family joke. For some reason, that little phrase wielded such leverage in securing small amounts of cash when even a remote connection to education could be made. Pat enjoyed school for the most part and did not have to be coerced into attending or studying. On the other hand, it was also nice that she could use the "it's for school" tag to acquire some of life's perks. This, of course, worked because her parents valued education and wanted to be sure that the children had all needed supplies for class, field trips, or projects. Thomas Lane, Jr.'s, education had largely consisted of informal apprenticeships under his father's tutelage. Although he was basically self-taught in the many areas in which he did well, he considered the provision of formal education for his children a top priority. Mabel Lane had enjoyed her high school years and shared stories of her experience with her children as they were growing up. She attributed equal import to her children's formal schooling; however, she did not fall victim to the "its for school" phrase as often as Pat's father.

Pat Lane

On February 3, 1970, Pat was sitting at the kitchen table of her Woodlane apartment having a cup of coffee and mentally preparing for the commute to work when she began perusing the *Mill Creek Star*. She had been keeping up with the events reported in the various newspapers concerning the dismantling of the Liberty Heights School District, but somehow that morning's headlines struck a nerve. "Orphan Black Students Adopted by Whites." Her response was that of her elderly grandmother, who still resided in the house on Adams Street in Liberty Heights. "Ain't that a blip!" It was an emotional response, but Pat actually found it difficult to remember and articulate the feelings from her seventh and eighth grade years that gave rise to the response. Much had been blocked and blurred; however, her memories of earlier school years were quite vivid.

Pat always knew that her family, the Lane Jr.'s, were not well off but were perhaps better off than other Black families in the valley. In fact, because she had so little to compare the family to, she reached adulthood believing that they were middle class. "Perhaps," she pondered to herself that day, "I was thinking average class." It was not until Pat was well into adulthood that she realized the error of her thinking, proving to her again that many things are relative. Growing up in one of the largest self-governed Black communities in the nation was unique in many ways, but most of her memories were extremely pleasant. Pat recalls that the first day she went off to kindergarten her biggest concern was being separated from her mother. What she remembers most vividly was coming home and telling her mother that she missed her. Pat was relieved to hear that her mother had missed her also. Her concern had stemmed from overhearing a friend of her mother say how nice it would be for her mother when Pat started school, that is to have all the kids out of the house. Her mother had agreed that it would be good to have some time to herself. Pat, of course, was appalled. She could not imagine her mother not wanting her to be clinging to her all day as Pat was in the habit of doing. As the youngest of three children, she was the last to venture off to Liberty Heights Elementary School. She soon stopped missing her mother and enjoyed many wonderful experiences there and later at the St. Althea Elementary School.

It was at St. Althea that Pat reached the seventh and eighth grades. The stress she felt during those years in the late 1950s was adult enough, but her stress management techniques were still so undeveloped. A new high school was built in Liberty Heights. It was scheduled to open soon, and Pat would have to go there. She understood that the school would have limited resources and would not offer the quality of education that her sister was presently enjoying. You see, prior to the construction of the new high school practically all school districts were open to the children of Liberty Heights. Since her sister would be entering her junior year in a public high school in another district, she would be allowed to complete her studies there. On the other hand, Pat and her brother, who is a year her senior, would have their options severely limited and would not take part in the open district benefits. The family was upset. Pat was upset.

Reading that morning's headlines brought up many questions—questions that had their roots in adolescence but nevertheless continued to haunt Pat as an adult. What events had led to this situation, which from her perspective was so unfortunate, so unfair? As she sat there at her kitchen table, more anxious feelings began to surface as she mentally returned to those adolescent years. Pat had internalized the view that education was the great equalizer and the sure means of attaining success. She did remember thinking at the time, "So why are my dreams being deferred, aspirations shattered, future doomed to mediocrity? Why is this happening to me?" However, like many other families who were concerned about the quality of education the new Liberty Heights High School might deliver, the Lanes found a solution to the problem in the parochial school system. Pat's anxieties were assuaged once she was successfully enrolled in Our Lady of the Hills High School in a wealthy suburb ten miles south of Liberty Heights.

Pat had many educational experiences since that time, for she had graduated from high school and college, but the turmoil that she felt in 1958–1959 still lurked in the corners of her memories. She still wanted to know why. She wanted to know who or what had put her hopes and the hopes of others in such jeopardy. She was currently pursuing, on a part-time basis, a graduate degree and was taking evening courses at a local state university campus. Glaring at the newspaper headlines that morning, Pat decided on the topic of her final project for that semester's course in educational research. She would explore the events of the 1950s in order to see if she could find some answers and finally put the issue to rest for herself. She was sure she would discover that the Liberty Heights school was built to keep Black Liberty Heights students there. She did not know if she would be able to document or validate her suspicions, but she was convinced that somehow the leaders in the community had failed its residents by either knowingly selling out to the segregationists (a yet-unidentified group in her mind), or they had unknowingly accepted monies disguised as "philanthropic gifts" that would lead to the further marginalization of the children and future citizens of Liberty Heights. She truly felt the situation that caused her so much distress was no accident and had somehow come about as a result of the manipulations of some group of White leaders intent on barring Liberty Heights students from their schools. Sure they were "rescuing" Liberty Heights now... in time for some perhaps but too late for others. "And why now?" was another question that began plaguing Pat that early February morning.

In attempting to gain insight into the historical background of her educational predicament, she looked at events that occurred during and just prior to that time period. Almost immediately she was led to accounts of the creation of Liberty Heights school district in 1950 and the creation of Liberty Heights as a city in 1951. From the documents examined, she gathered that the intents of these events were not to benefit Liberty Heights. She began stepping back into history. What was in the master plan of 1948 for the greater metropolitan area that influenced the events of 1950 and 1951? Did the economic land use and motorways plans drafted by the same commission have an effect? What, if any, effect did the developments in 1935 under Roosevelt's greenbelt project have on Liberty Heights and what factors led to this project? The more research Pat did, the further she had to go back in history to try to establish the origin and nature of the attitudes of those who had so profoundly affected her. In studying the case of Liberty Heights she would also uncover the history and nature of the "benevolent" Price Valley rescuer. Her backward steps landed her in the nineteenth century. It is from there that she began in order to proceed to 1958.

PART II

The Fly

CHAPTER 2

Segregation by Gerrymander: The Creation of the Lincoln Heights (Ohio) School District

This chapter is an historical case study tracing the formation of a school district profoundly influenced by racial, political, sociological, and economic factors. The analysis of the racial, political, and economic environments prevailing in Cincinnati, Ohio, from the turn of the century through the 1950s illuminates the formation of a school district serving a predominately low-income Black community and student body. This investigation shows how economic factors influenced the formation of cities and communities and how the formation of school districts was intricately tied to this evolution. Furthermore, it confirms the relationship between economic participation and educational opportunities and explains the causes of the emergence of race and class-segregated communities and school districts.

Introduction

Historical Background

As Carter (1995) and Russo, Harris, and Sandidge (1994) point out, the educational system in the United States historically has failed to provide equal access to all citizens. Evidence of this failure is found, and somewhat explained, in the research literature that points convincingly to a link between the nation's educational and economic systems. (Becker, 1964; Bowman, 1991; Weiss, 1995) Such a relationship, by its very nature, inhibits the equality of educational opportunities available to all Americans. For example, as outlined by Bowman (1991), the association between educational attainment and economic status supports the notion that a positive and reciprocal relationship exists between the level of participation in the economic system and level of access to quality education. One underlying premise of the research detailed in this chapter is that this linkage has served to disenfranchise the Black American from slavery to citizenship and from past to present.

During slavery, the relationship between economic participation and educational opportunity was obvious. Efforts to teach Black slaves to read and write were virtually nonexistent. The slave participated in the economic system not as an individual entity with the rights, privileges, and benefits accorded free citizens but rather as an inanimate cog in the production process at worst and as an agent to a privileged individual at best. Although there were groups, such as the Quakers, who extended opportunities to Blacks, the larger society denied slaves personal access to goods and services. If the Black slave's duties required literacy, then, and typically only then, the slaveowner would provide the appropriate training and education. Webber (1978) chronicles such a case in his work on slave education between 1831 and 1865. As he notes:

> Some few masters appear to have taken an active interest in the education of a select few slaves. J. H. Curry's father was taught to read and write by his master who was a doctor so that he could take the addresses of visiting patients. (p. 132)

The end of the Civil War brought large numbers of Blacks to urban areas seeking the American Dream. However, White Americans, including those whose political and military stances brought an end to physical bondage, were not willing to allow Blacks full participation in the economic system. Because of low wages and the intermittent absence of income, the Black residents of the urban centers could afford only the worst living quarters, and educational opportunities for Black children were still scarce. After the Civil War and during Reconstruction, Blacks played a larger role in the economic organizations and structures. As would be predicted by the relationship between economic and educational participation hypothesized above, Black residents also created and partook of increased educational opportunities. Washington (1901) attests to this phenomenon in personal observations recorded during this era:

> Few people who were not right in the midst of the scenes can form any exact idea of the intense desire which the people of my race showed for an education....It was a whole race trying to go to school....Day-school, night-school, Sunday-school, were always crowded, and often many had to be turned away for want of room. (p. 30)

Though Reconstruction was short lived, it demonstrated the existence of a positive relationship between the economic and educational systems. When Congress restored political rights and powers to the ex-Confederates, Urban and Wagoner (1996) contend that it removed or seriously compromised the temporary enfranchisement of Black Americans.

Perhaps these diminished expectations of social systems and institutions explain Booker T. Washington's commitment to the concept of industrial (or vocational) education as manifested by his work at Tuskegee Institute in Alabama. According to Washington (1901), the institute's founders aimed to give Tuskegee students "such a practical knowledge of some one industry, together with the spirit of industry, thrift, and economy, that they would be sure of knowing how to make a living after they had left us." (p. 126) Surmising that White employers would deny the newly freed Blacks jobs that required a liberal arts education, Washington speculated that the same controlling powers would deny such an education to Blacks. Indeed, Washington's most compelling reality was that "a vocational education was all that the larger, White-dominated society would allow." (Dunn, 1993, p. 27) Aware of job discrimination practices, he maintained that Blacks should seek economic freedom and autonomy by preparing for the jobs that would most likely be open to them. Thus, in this way, the expected level of accessibility to the economic system influenced the quality and type of education provided to and sought by Black Americans.

A biographical sketch of Black Cincinnatian Richard Cammack, whose family moved to Ohio in 1869, further demonstrates the influence of economic position upon educational opportunity. (Dabney, 1926) As Dabney writes:

> Negro schooling was very scarce in those days. Young Cammack got a little of it. The schools for "colored" were only open a few months. The school board would say, "You Negroes don't pay enough taxes to have schools like white folks." (p. 239)

W. E. B. Du Bois (1903) roundly criticized Washington's emphasis on industrial education for Blacks, refusing to accept the realities that Washington attempted to circumvent. By his estimation, "If we make money the object of man-training, we shall develop money-makers but not necessarily men; if we make technical skill the object of education, we may possess artisans but not, in nature, men." (p. 31) Du Bois's views paralleled those of many middle- and upper-class White citizens in various sections of the country who argued for and sought a quality liberal arts education for their children, most of whom were educated in private schools. (Synnott, 1979) Among these Whites, it was widely believed that such an education would ensure these students' economic participation in the system on par with that of their parents. For those Blacks who agreed with Du Bois's view, a liberal arts education was seen as the principal route to personal, political, social, and economic uplift.

With the growing emphasis on industrial growth, the curricula and methodologies of the public school, which was largely consigned to the children of the lower and working classes, began to emulate the factory model, thereby locking these young citizens into their parents' lower socioeconomic status. Not only did the demands of factory life influence school curricula and methodologies, businessmen ran and controlled the reorganized school boards. (Callahan, 1962) Clearly, by strongly supporting the drive for vocational education, many of these business leaders saw the educational system as a tool for training future laborers. They emphasized the implementation of cost-effective practices and efficiency principles in the schools so that these institutions would more closely respond to the needs of the nation's business community. Subsequently, White working-class citizens who took full advantage of the public educational opportunity, whatever its limitations, could at least maintain their utilitarian position in the economic system. The Black worker, however, was often denied even the opportunity to attend public schools. (Sundstrom, 1994)

Businessmen who discriminated against Blacks in their hiring and promotion practices saw education for Blacks and other non-White citizens as a waste of resources. Their resistance to the idea of expending educational resources on individuals they deemed not likely to benefit from such resources increased after the 1909 publication of Leonard Ayres's book, *Laggards in Our Schools*. As Callahan (1962) attests:

> Certainly Ayres' book, together with other developments…helped set the stage for the spectacular debut of the efficiency expert on the American scene in the fall of 1910….[S]chool administrators, under constant pressure to make education more practical in order to serve a business society better, were brought under even stronger criticism and forced to demonstrate first, last, and always that they were operating the schools efficiently. (p. 18)

During the years of massive economic depression in the late 1920s and 1930s, concerns for efficiency continued to pervade the U.S. educational system, further influencing the curricula, methodologies, and policies applied. By the time the Great Depression exerted its full effect upon American society, urban Blacks occupied the lowest rung on the socioeconomic ladder and were overwhelmingly locked in the lowest-paying jobs and the most substandard housing. As Sundstrom (1994) explains, "Blacks who migrated to the North found improved economic opportunities, but job segregation remained significant. Indeed, in 1910 the relative underrepresentation of blacks in the crafts and industrial operative jobs was greater in the North than the South." (p. 384) According to Urban and Wagoner (1996), "the economic suffering of these groups during the 1920s was also accompanied by a substantial degree of educational deprivation...[a]nd Black Americans suffered, both economically and educationally, even more than their white working-class or farm counterparts." (p. 242)

Disparities such as those noted may well have been linked to the efforts of city planners to segregate the populations of their municipalities along racial lines during the early twentieth century. (Taylor, 1993) With Blacks relegated to low-income communities, school boards were free to establish districts with minimal and substandard resources, accomplishing de facto segregation without the appearance of malice. Given that urban schools were often supported by local taxes, the tax valuation of a district was considered a significant index of the level of education that could be provided. (Miami University, Bureau of Educational Field Services, 1961) City planners thus set in motion a cycle that would compromise Black students' futures for generations.

The pattern of inferior elementary and secondary education established during these early years of public schooling would limit the types of jobs accessible to Blacks, thereby giving employers a ready excuse for denying Black applicants the more skilled and higher-paid positions that might raise Black citizens' standards of living. By design, schools in poorer districts populated by Blacks lacked college preparatory curricula, thus limiting chances for college or university entrance by either certificate or examination. (Synnott, 1979) Further, the inadequate preparation afforded Black students jeopardized their chances of being accepted into institutions of higher learning. Moreover, Black parents' limited economic opportunities in many cases guaranteed that they could not afford college for their children. Thus, the cycle continued through generations of parents, children, grandchildren, and so forth, establishing both a reciprocal linkage and a positively correlated relationship between economics, race, and education that has endured throughout U.S. history.

Statement of Purpose

This chapter traces the formation of a specific urban school district that was clearly and profoundly influenced by political, sociological, and, most important, economic factors. Its purpose is threefold: (a) to provide an historical case study that confirms the relationship between economic participation and educational opportunity; (b) to elucidate the causes underlying the emergence of race- and class-segregated communities and school districts; and (c) to bring into focus the disenfranchisement this relationship has engendered in the Black community. Specifically, this study analyzes the racial, political, and economic environments that prevailed in Cincinnati, Ohio, from the turn of the century through the 1950s that led to the creation of the Lincoln Heights school district and high school, which served a predominantly low-income Black community.

The case of Cincinnati's Lincoln Heights community presents a rare opportunity to trace the emergence of a racially segregated community and school district contiguous with city lines. How this community came to be nestled among, yet cut off from, valuable resources and individuals with access to resources warrants investigation. How Lincoln Heights high school students moved from racially integrated schools and classrooms to an almost totally segregated school environment also warrants investigation. As educational historians contend, current situations often yield more information in light of, or relative to, past events or trends. (Borg & Gall, 1989) Thus, it is hoped that this examination will elucidate the long-term impact of denied economic access at the community level upon individual educational opportunity. The underlying assumption of the study is that the phenomena uncovered may be typical of other urban-industrial areas across the nation.

On the Study's Methodology

The historical case study method used in this research marshals comprehensive data that bring into sharper focus the matrix of economics and education as well as that of race and class and that explain the evolution of these matrices in an urban-industrial Midwestern U.S. city. In keeping with historical research techniques, data were discovered, rather than created, in books, journals, reports, city plans, and other primary and secondary sources. The data are presented in chronological order and in a narrative format.

This historical investigation uncovered evidence that Cincinnati, Ohio, officials manipulated the Lincoln Heights city lines in a process similar to gerrymandering. (Cranor, Crawley, & Scheele, 1989) In its broad sense, gerrymandering means any tinkering with municipal or district lines to obtain some advantage or position of power. (Roget, 1994) The term is often used when voting districts are manipulated to award electoral advantage to a particular person or political party. (Bernstein, 1996) However, in the creation of Lincoln Heights High School, the manipulation of city lines severely limited the Lincoln Heights community's economic resources and awarded economic advantages to neighboring communities. This economic gerrymandering also created a racially segregated city, school district, and high school.

The Case of Lincoln Heights

In 1950, the Lincoln Heights community was comprised of a poor Black populace and was surrounded by wealthy communities and rich industrial areas just outside its borders. (Miami University, Bureau of Educational Field Services, 1961) Prior to 1958, there was no public high school in Lincoln Heights, and the children of this community attended schools with varying ratios of White and Black enrollments in districts throughout the Cincinnati area. In that year, Lincoln Heights High School (LHHS) was completed, and with the exception of junior- or senior-level students who had begun their studies elsewhere, the majority of Lincoln Heights children attended the new school. Essentially, however, LHHS served to segregate rather than desegregate its students even after the 1954 *Brown v. Board of Education of Topeka, Kansas* decision.

Education in Cincinnati during the Preindustrial Era

Historical accounts published as early as the 1920s look back at schooling for Cincinnati's Black residents in the antebellum period and find it virtually nonexistent. Dabney (1926) gives a chilling account of the violent birth and necessarily clandestine spread of educational institutions for Blacks in this emerging midwestern commercial and industrial center. According to his reports, White teachers from Oberlin College traveled to nearby Cincinnati ex-

pressly to teach Black children. These teachers, who generally held aboli-
tionist views, endured the animosity and oftentimes the mob threats of their
opponents. The original student body of Oberlin College consisted of those
who had abandoned Lane Seminary in Cincinnati subsequent to the order
that forbade the discussion of slavery. (Dabney, 1926; Fletcher, 1943) Au-
thorities issued the order after groups of citizens stormed school grounds to
protest such discussions. When teachers from Oberlin began their mission-
ary journeys to Cincinnati, the threats followed them. Their identities were
made known locally, and White merchants often refused to provide lodging
and other services. (Dabney, 1926) Buildings where instruction took place
attracted riot-like behavior and threats of burning. Establishments that might
have otherwise offered space for classrooms were thus discouraged from
doing so.

Such were the prevailing attitudes in preindustrial Cincinnati. A closer
look uncovers political, social, and economic dynamics also relevant to the
history of Black education in this city. For example, "[w]hen the General
Assembly incorporated Cincinnati as a city in 1819, the state conferred an
expected and deserved distinction upon the most important urban center in
the valley. From a squalid river settlement, Cincinnati had been transformed
into a commercial mart of ten thousand people, and its phenomenal growth
during the next 19 years seemed to justify the action of the legislature."
(Aaron, 1992)

Prior to industrialization, Cincinnati had been an important commercial
center on the banks of the Ohio River. In describing the Cincinnati of 1847,
Dabney (1926) states,

> It is situated on the north bank of the Ohio river, opposite the mouth of the Licking
> river, which enters the Ohio between Newport and Covington, Kentucky. This city
> is near the eastern extremity of a valley about twelve miles in circumference, sur-
> rounded by beautiful hills, which rise to the height of 300 feet by gentle and varying
> slopes, and mostly covered with native forest trees. (p. 16)

The city's spontaneous, amoeba-like growth came about as a direct result of increasing steamboat traffic as well as the heightened buying, selling,
and trading of goods along the Ohio River and the opening of numerous
shops of various kinds. (Aaron, 1992) During the early 1800s, Cincinnati
had no city planning commissions, zoning laws, or building codes (Taylor,
1993), and the law of supply and demand seemed to direct growth. The

city's center was relatively small in area and limited by its very terrain, which proved of critical importance as Cincinnati entered the industrial era and experienced tremendous population growth. This growth restriction directly affected municipal building policies, which, in turn, limited both residential space for new inhabitants and commercial space for new factories, offices, and businesses. The commercial center eventually expanded into the industrial center, exhausting all available space within the river and creek beds and at the base of the hills. However, inadequate transportation left the city's workforce without efficient means of daily travel over these terrain barriers.

Blacks, Whites, immigrants, businesses, and factories competed for the same space during these early years of Cincinnati's history. (Taylor, 1984, 1993) This is an important factor to consider when analyzing racial attitudes and the ways these attitudes promoted the growth of urban racial ghettoes in general and the emergence of Lincoln Heights in particular.

The outcome of the Civil War, coupled with the rise of industrialization, had the same general effects on urban areas throughout the United States. The failed farms in the nation's rural areas prompted Blacks and Whites to seek new opportunities en masse in centers such as Cincinnati. According to Urban and Wagoner (1996): "Some blacks, keenly aware of the deteriorating conditions surrounding their tenuous freedom, joined in an 'exodus' from the South." (p. 151) However, because of the lack of residential space in Cincinnati's industrial center in the early 1900s, Whites, Blacks, and immigrants of various origins lived in close proximity to each other. By Taylor's (1993) account, due to lack of space rather than a lack of racial animosity or discriminatory practices at the time, Blacks were not segregated in certain segments of the city or even specific streets. Other historians report the prevalence of job discrimination practices in factories and businesses. For example, Sundstrom (1994) states,

> It is well known that blacks were underrepresented in the more skilled and higher-paid jobs…[and] in the…professional, and clerical categories in both the North and the South. The virtual exclusion of black women from clerical and sales jobs is notable. (p. 385)

Not only did White employers hire Black Cincinnatians for the lowest-paying jobs and deny them upward movement, White fellow laborers expressed a reluctance to work alongside Blacks, which heightened tensions.

Dabney (1926) contends that these tensions were prevalent in Cincinnati from 1826 to 1840 and states:

> White laborers there, as in other Northern cities during this period, easily reached the position of thinking that it was a disgrace to work with Negroes. This prejudice was so much more inconvenient to the Negroes of Cincinnati than elsewhere because most of the menial labor in that city was done by Germans and Irishmen. Since the Negroes could not follow ordinary menial occupations there was nothing left for them but the lowest form of "drudgery," for which employers often preferred colored women. (p. 34)

Taylor (1984) depicts the city's early commercial area through the use of maps. These maps reveal that although Black Cincinnatians were not as yet segregated during this preindustrial stage, they tended to live in clusters interspersed among the working class and occupied the worst living quarters in any particular section of town or on any street. Taylor argues that segregation and the rise of the ghetto slum developed only after transportation advances allowed Cincinnati's population to traverse terrain barriers efficiently. These advances also freed city officials to incorporate racial preferences into their building policies. These critical developments occurred between 1910 and 1940.

The Era of Outward Migration

The overcrowded and squalid conditions of Cincinnati's tenements captured the attention of housing reformers and led to the passage of a building code in 1898, which was strengthened in 1916. Reformers also sought to encourage workers to move out of the river basin area of the city into the hilltop and valley areas that were becoming more accessible because of advances in transportation. These advances also opened up areas for new factories and businesses away from the banks of the Ohio River and the original industrial core, and residents sought to move closer to newly accessible job sites.

Taylor (1993) points out that in the 1920s it was mainly White workers who moved out of the Cincinnati basin, encouraged by a newly organized group of city planners called the Better Housing League (BHL). This left behind practically the entire Black Cincinnati population and thereby set in motion the emergence of a segregated Black ghetto in the city's West End. Subsequent job and housing discrimination rendered Black migration outward from this basin area next to impossible, and most Blacks could not afford the single-family homes being erected in the hilltop and valley areas. As Whites abandoned the "superior" living units in the West End, the members of the BHL believed these units would default to the remaining Black residents.

Taylor (1993) recounts a specific incident in 1924 in which city planners advised a charitable group of Cincinnatians, whose primary concern was relieving the plight of the Black slum dweller, to subscribe to this trickle-down housing philosophy. Accordingly, BHL members informed Blacks and their supporters that it was "impossible to build houses directly for the colored people because the facts show that their wages are insufficient to pay the cost of present-day construction." (p. 176) They next suggested that friends of African Americans should be encouraged to invest their money in the building of new houses for Whites. "This," they indicated, "while not relieving colored families directly would tend to relieve them indirectly by drawing white families out of the district now occupied for the most part by colored people." (p. 176) Thus, confinement to the basin area and to housing vacated as a result of White flight became the cornerstones of the BHL's strategy for dealing with the Black housing problem.

In the minds of White Cincinnatians of the day, the squalid conditions of the West End were so intricately linked to its Black residents that the place and the people were synonymous. (Taylor, 1993) Whites believed that Blacks naturally gravitated to such conditions and held Blacks themselves responsible for the conditions that were, in reality, forced upon them. Thus, White city officials and citizens supported several methods—formal, informal, direct, and indirect—of curtailing the movements of Black Cincinnatians, whom many Whites believed would likely bring the slums with them if allowed to relocate. City ordinances were passed that prohibited real estate developers from selling lots to and building houses for Blacks outside the basin. The new White homeowners in the outlying hilltop and valley areas supported these racist policies, believing that they were protecting their investments.

Officials also used mortgage-lending practices to contain Black movement in flourishing Cincinnati. Typically, in the post-WWI era mortgage loans were granted by banks for a period of two to five years and were not renewed automatically. Renewal depended in part on the property in question maintaining its original value. Failure to attain loan renewal would mean that the resident would lose the home and perhaps all that had been invested. (Taylor, 1993, p. 167) As more working-class White Cincinnatians became homeowners, they, too, became more concerned with property values. The majority of them also came to view Blacks and slums as inseparably linked, and they adamantly supported segregated neighborhoods in the belief that they were safeguarding their property values. Use of public monies also restricted Black relocation. Federal money available for public housing projects, for example, was earmarked to rescue the deserving. (Miller, 1981) It was thus expedient for Whites to believe that Blacks created slum environments and were, therefore, undeserving of better housing conditions.

Finally, during this post-WWI period Cincinnati passed zoning laws and building codes and adopted development plans that curtailed the spread of slums. The few Blacks who, against all odds, secured land in the developing areas could only afford to build shacks, which were seen as a scourge and a threat to the future of Cincinnati. These shacks also reinforced negative attitudes about Black residents. In 1923, Cincinnati enacted its first zoning laws controlling the quality and types of structures that could be built in various parts of the city. These laws further inhibited the outward migration of Black residents from the basin. Two years later, the Cincinnati City Planning Commission (1925) published the first city plan, which incorporated the same principles that had guided the previously established building codes and zoning laws:

> The colored population is continuing to increase fairly rapidly, while the number of houses in which they may live is remaining stationary. Nearly 3,500 new colored people have come into Cincinnati since 1920. This is bound to remain a problem for several decades to come. (p. 50)

Actually, 18,000 additional Blacks had moved to Cincinnati by 1920. (Taylor, 1993) Most of these residents occupied the already-crowded West End basin area, this being virtually their only option. Taylor (1993) cites zoning laws and building codes as major contributors to the rise of what was fast and, by design, a major ghetto slum. He makes a strong case for this assertion by pointing out that although extreme racism had existed in Cincinnati for years, it was not until certain city planning, zoning, and residential building laws incorporated this racism into municipal edicts that the ghetto slum emerged. Specifically, he notes that the BHL's trickle-down housing philosophy found its way into the text of the 1925 city plan almost verbatim:

The only way in which the housing shortage can be substantially relieved is by producing more homes. Single-family houses cannot be built to sell for less than
$5,000, including the land....It is therefore obvious that the construction of single-
family houses cannot meet the needs of the mass of the colored population and the
white low-wage earners....[T]he only way housing accommodations can be provided for them is by relieving the pressure higher up. In other words, as fast as the families in better circumstance move out of the older tenements and houses, they will
become available for housing the lower wage earners. This means that it is not feasi-
ble now to give any consideration as a part of the City Plan to providing housing for
low-wage earners, and that attention should be concentrated now on the ameliora-
tion of living conditions in the older parts of town by zoning protection and by the
provision of parks, playgrounds, community centers and open spaces. (Cincinnati
City Planning Commission, 1925, p. 51)

The Commission's plan also illuminated the relationship between the
city planners and the local boards of education by indicating which schools
would be eliminated as well as where new schools would be located. Clearly, these city planners believed they had not only superior access to relevant
knowledge but also greater wisdom to designate school locations and school
districts. As their plan maintains:

[W]ith the limited data on population growth and distribution that the Board of
Education can normally have at its disposal, it is impossible for them to prognosti-
cate the rate and distribution of future growth as accurately as can a City Planning
Commission....It is the function of a City Planning Commission to determine the location and districts, public buildings and other features of the City Plan in the best
interest of the community as a whole. (p. 182)

It is likely, however, that these same discriminatory public plans and
policies yielded an unanticipated result: the birth of a Black haven, a community located away from the West End, that ultimately became the city of
Lincoln Heights. The history of that section is the focus of the subsequent
discussion.

The Upper Valley

In 1923, the Haley Livingston Land Company, contrary to accepted policy,
sold to Blacks plots of land north of the industrial center in what was known
as Lockland or Cincinnati's upper valley, and thus offered numbers of Black
Cincinnatians the option of living in an area other than the devitalized, con-
gested West End. The new residents erected homes on the land, which was

identified as tract C30A in the 1940 Census and later became known as Lincoln Heights. (U.S. Department of Commerce, Bureau of the Census, 1940) However, because of their owners' limited funds, these residential structures did not meet the standards of city planners and housing reformers. Taylor (1993) describes the White city leaders' perceptions of these dwellings, noting, for example, that the BHL's Standish Meacham referred to them as "bad Spots" and potential slums and called the black suburb "the ugliest collection of shacks [he had] ever seen." (p. 175) The director of buildings for the city, Clifford M. Stegner, called the new Black residential settlement a "menace to the city." (p. 175) Despite these negative attitudes, the Lincoln Heights community grew and improved over the years. Remaining close to 100% Black, it became one of the largest African American communities in the nation. Yet, Lincoln Heights remained poor relative to its neighboring White communities and continued to draw their criticism.

Without benefit of formal city planning or federal development monies, Lincoln Heights developed in geographic proximity to three more affluent White communities. As shown in Figure 1, the new settlement was located south of Woodlawn, a community that separates it from the wealthy Glendale area, and east of Greenhills, a community that was funded and developed under President Franklin D. Roosevelt's "greenbelt" initiative. Initiated in 1935 and operated under the auspices of the federal Resettlement Administration, this program was an attempt to relieve overcrowding in cities by establishing communities in fertile rural land on the outskirts of cities. (Miller, 1981) The program's developers hoped to rescue those trapped in the slums and provide a means of escape for the inhabitants of the era's numerous failed farms, who would likely migrate to more industrial areas.

Specifically, the program stipulated that protected parks or forests must surround or lie adjacent to the new communities; these protected areas would allow for controlled growth and prevent overpopulation. Cincinnati was one of three cities funded by the Resettlement Administration to develop such a community.

Greenhills was chartered as a municipality in 1939. According to Miller (1981):

> Greenhills was located on a 5,930-acre tract of farmland eleven miles north of downtown Cincinnati, in Springfield Township, Hamilton County, Ohio. The site lay northeast of Mt. Healthy and west of Glendale, a nineteenth century commuter suburb and the home of some of the wealthiest and most influential people, but not far either from the factories of Mill Creek industrial belt. (p. 7)

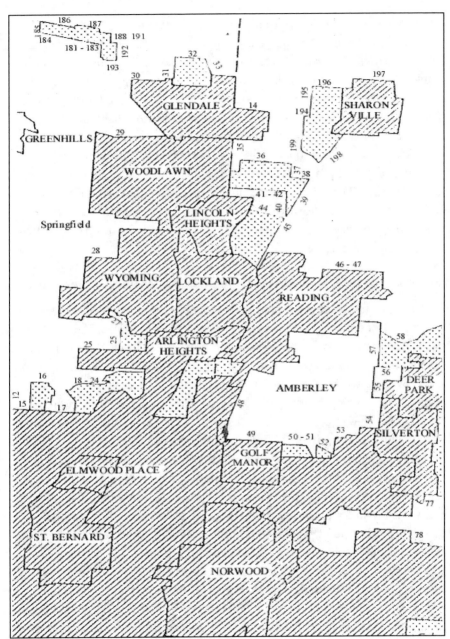

Figure 1. Cincinnati's Upper Valley Region.

Source: U.S. Department of Commerce, Bureau of the Census, 1950.

On one hand, this description of the new community's location and appearance suggests that it could be considered among the greenbelt program's successes. On the other hand, the racial makeup of the Greenhills community suggests that it had fallen short of a key program objective. As Miller continues: "In the 1940s the town developed into a white, middle-income suburb, despite the fact that Cincinnati's slums, whose inhabitants were supposed to be among Greenhills' major beneficiaries, contained large numbers of blacks." (p. 8) Indeed, the 1940 Census reported 718 occupied units, with one unit occupied by non-Whites. (U.S. Department of Commerce, Bureau of the Census, 1940) Details were not reported for what would become the Lincoln Heights area; however, the 1950 Census reported 1,328 occupied units in that community, with 1,305 occupied by non-Whites. (U.S. Department of Commerce, Bureau of the Census, 1950)

The Impact of the Cincinnati Metropolitan Master Plan of 1948

Plans for the future development and expansion of the Greenhills area reflected the principles underlying the Cincinnati Metropolitan Master Plan of 1948. (Cincinnati City Planning Commission, 1948) That plan reorganized the city into self-contained communities of 20,000 to 40,000 inhabitants connected by a network of highways. It specified sites for public housing and for industrial development, keeping residential areas separate from industrial areas. Other plan objectives included slum clearance and the introduction of federal public housing in the Greenhills area. (Miller,1981)

Attitudes concerning housing for Blacks as expicitly articulated in the 1925 plan differed little from those implicit in the 1948 master plan. Nonetheless, three key developments exemplify the extent to which Blacks benefited from the latter plan. The first occurred amid efforts by city leaders in 1951 and 1952 to purchase the Greenhills community and surrounding properties from the government and to expand and develop the northern Greenhills area. Those Cincinnati leaders committed to these efforts included many of the leaders who developed the 1948 plan. As documented by Miller (1981), memoranda and interview records confirm that this leadership was well aware that the expressway system proposed in their plan would dislocate a large portion of the residents of the Black West End. Despite acknowledgment of this fact, however, these leaders did not offer relocation to housing to the group most at risk. Miller concludes: "The implication seems clear. North Greenhills would not provide housing for blacks uprooted from

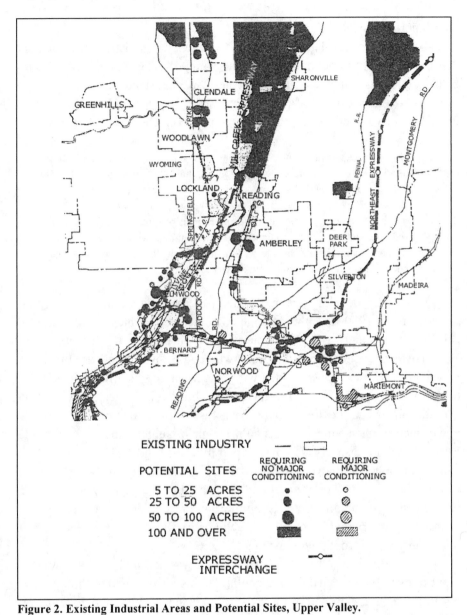

Figure 2. Existing Industrial Areas and Potential Sites, Upper Valley.
Source: Cincinnati City Planning Commission, *The Cincinnati Metropolitan Master Plan and the Official City Plan of Cincinnati, 1948.*

their inner-city neighborhoods." (p. 20)

The 1948 master plan slated areas for intensive industrial development that were adjacent to but outside of what would soon become the city of Lincoln Heights—an unlabeled area just north of Lockland on Figure 2. The Miami University Bureau of Educational Field Services study delineates the impact of the new industrial locations upon Lincoln Heights:

> In 1946, after deleting the industrial portion of the territory sought, the County Commissioners granted incorporation to a total land area of 0.804 square miles. By 1950, the Federal Census showed a population of at least five thousand. City status was imminent. But efforts to annex valuable industrial property were blocked, and in 1951, when Evandale incorporated, Lincoln Heights became land-locked in a rich industrial area without a further chance for expansion and without opportunity to share proportionately in the taxable wealth of the industrial community. (Miami University, Bureau of Educational Field Services, 1961, p. 6)

This last key development punctuated Lincoln Heights' incorporation into a village. In 1950, by either strange coincidence or strategic intent, the local Hamilton County Board of Education, upon petition by the citizens of Woodlawn, abolished the old Woodlawn school district and established a new district whose lines coincided with that community's village lines. Prior to this action, many Lincoln Heights schoolchildren had attended schools in Woodlawn, for the previous school district overlapped the boundaries of the newly incorporated village of Lincoln Heights. Neighboring Lockland and Evandale school districts also overlapped those of Lincoln Heights. Technically, although Woodlawn redefined its school district to exclude properties in Lincoln Heights, the latter should not have been designated as having a school district coinciding with its corporation lines because of the remaining overlapping districts. However, this technicality did not prevent the Hamilton County board from doing just that.

Evidence indicates that the board's action was accomplished without the input or even the knowledge of Lincoln Heights citizens and without adhering to procedures outlined in the existing Cincinnati municipal code. Legal notice of the new Lincoln Heights school district appeared in the *Cincinnati Post* newspaper, but this notice "failed to mention that a remonstrance petition filed by the qualified majority of electors in the district could prevent the action." (Miami University, Bureau of Educational Field Services, 1961, p. 12) In reference to the problem of overlapping city and district lines, "[t]he code required a map to be filed with the County Auditor as a part of the procedure in creating a school district. At the time of this writing…this map could not be located in the Hamilton County Auditor's files." (Miami University, Bureau of Educational Field Services, 1961, p. 11) The Miami University Bureau of Educational Field Services concluded its analysis of this redistricting as follows:

> There are some who hold the belief that the birth of Lincoln Heights city school district was the result of pre-conceived effort to place the school district in this position to force independence, that this action was taken prematurely, and that this action was taken with no legal compulsion. Furthermore, too little consideration was given to the financial structure for future operation. (p. 13)

The above-noted irregularities did not escape the notice of Harris and Erickson (1951) in their study of school consolidation in Hamilton County. Their comments warrant their near-complete inclusion here:

> The petition to create two new districts, Woodlawn and Lincoln Heights, which was approved by the County Board, provided for the withdrawal of only 17% of the pupils into the new Woodlawn district, but left only 46% of the tax valuation to support the remaining 83% of the pupils. The withdrawing area now has a ration of $8,801 per child, while the remaining area has only the incredibly low ration of $1,544 per child. It is to be noted that it is this withdrawing area, with the high valuation, which is still a part of the county system, while the municipality of Lincoln Heights, with its low valuation, is the area which is expected to become a city school district and therefore no longer a concern of the county school board. The motives which this set of facts seems to impute to the county board are hardly very commendable. There is also the possibility of a racial question. The district before division was largely colored; after separation the new Woodlawn area was little less than half colored (in school enrollments) while Lincoln Heights was entirely colored. There are indications here that the white minority pulled out, taking with them the bulk of the wealth, in order to become a majority in the new Woodlawn district. For school purposes, the result of this division has been that a populous but impoverished area has been cut loose from the county system and left isolated to meet alone almost insuperable obstacles to financing an adequate educational system. This is the complete opposite of the basic principle of consolidation, which is to join small and financially insufficient areas so that better and more economical education can be achieved. (pp. 66–67)

The Creation of the Lincoln Heights School District

Once it became a separate school district, the village of Lincoln Heights

needed its own high school. The Ohio State Department of Education granted the community a high school charter in April 1958. By September of that
year, a 240-pupil, four-year high school bearing the Lincoln Heights name
was opened. A new city had been established, a new school district created,
and a new high school built, but the new school building could not obscure
the fact that most Lincoln Heights High School (LHHS) students struggled
along with fewer textbooks, libraries, and seasoned teachers compared to
their White peers in the wealthier neighboring districts. For these reasons,
some Black parents continued to send their children to schools outside the
district, on a tuition basis, bearing the cost themselves. (Miami University,
Bureau of Educational Field Services, 1961)

Documentation of comparative tax valuations of these more affluent districts shortly after the opening of LHHS indicates the resources schools
within those districts could afford. The Miami University Bureau of Educational Field Services (1961) provides this information and points out its rele-
vance by stating the following:

> The tax valuation of a school district constitutes an important index of ability to pro-
> vide a good educational program....The relationship of the number of pupils to the
> total tax valuation is also significant. The smaller the number of enrolled pupils, the
> larger the amount of money per pupil available from tax revenues for educational
> purposes. (p. 107)

The Miami University Bureau of Educational Field Services also com-
pares Lincoln Heights' tax valuation per pupil with that of other districts in
the state and county. As they note:

> In 1960, the tax valuation per pupil was $7,667, a figure which compares very unfa-
> vorably with other districts in Ohio....In 1960 the average per pupil wealth was
> $17,583 for all city school districts, $10,648 for all exempted village school dis-
> tricts, $11,406 for all local school districts in county systems, and $15,042...for all
> districts in the state. Lincoln Heights has only half the ability (50.7 per cent) to sup-
> port an educational program through local taxes that the average district in Ohio
> has....In Hamilton County itself, Lincoln Heights ranks, in tax valuation per pupil,
> lowest of the ten city school districts....St. Bernard is first with $114,963, and
> Lock-land is second with $55,632....Lincoln Heights also has a lower valuation per
> pupil than any of the eight local school districts in Hamilton County...or than any of
> the exempted villages in the county. (p. 109)

Thus, the struggle with fewer resources and the emergence of the school district that brought about this struggle provide evidence of more than simply the reciprocal correlation between economic participation and educational opportunities. These factors also make obvious the disenfranchisement this relationship engendered in the Black Cincinnati community. Although LHHS can boast of many successful graduates who, with the help of dedicated educators, overcame many obstacles, one can only wonder how many more Black Cincinnatians would have enjoyed fuller adult lives if their paths had not been determined by these external factors.

Conclusion

I have great faith in the power and influence of facts. It is seldom that anything is permanently gained by holding back a fact. (Booker T. Washington, 1901, p. 32)

The hidden economic and political forces that gave rise to the school district serving Lincoln Heights' children actually determined the paths and patterns of their lives. In a nation where many espouse the virtues of rugged individualism and self-empowerment, it is important to expose those often overwhelming but hidden forces that are external to the individual and that oppose self-empowerment and agency. Perhaps the adult citizens of Lincoln Heights could have been more diligent and vigilant in determining and protecting their rights and preventing the gerrymandering of their community and school district. However, the history of oppression in this urban area, as chronicled in this chapter, strongly suggests that Lincoln Heights' Black residents were not privy to the boardroom decisions that would have allowed them to act in a timely or appropriate manner to resist these outside interventions.

Evidence indicates that the events of 1950 and 1951 were controlled by Cincinnati city planners and the Hamilton County Board of Education and that the major outcome of these events—the building of Lincoln Heights High School—was forced upon the residents of the community. If the Black inhabitants of this unique urban community had been able to afford to construct dwellings that conformed with city standards and zoning requirements, perhaps they would have been deemed worthy of federal assistance like their Greenhills neighbors to the west. However, White city officials viewed Lincoln Heights inhabitants as solely responsible for their depressed surroundings and expected that they would re-create their "natural" habitat of impoverished settings no matter where they located. Because of these prevailing negative attitudes, investment, municipal or otherwise, in Lincoln Heights was considered unwise, and the road most frequently taken was to contain this Black community. If surrounding locales could wrest themselves from association with Lincoln Heights, barring ownership or free access to economic and educational resources, then that containment would be complete. By establishing Lincoln Heights as a separate city, excluding from its boundaries valuable industrial properties, and establishing a school district that was subsequently deprived of the substantial tax revenues generated by the businesses removed from its midst, the city planners' mission was accomplished.

Believing that education is the great equalizer and yet suspecting that access to quality education is unequal are not paradoxical. This research process has illuminated and provided deeper understandings of both notions. Uncovering the truth, regardless of how repugnant, has simultaneously informed, enlightened, and liberated the researcher. The implications for further study are numerous. Tracing the formation of other racially segregated communities and school districts, using a multiple-case-study approach, would help determine whether the events that occurred in the greater Cincinnati area from the 1900s through the 1950s are representative of community and school district formation across the nation. Expanding such research into the 1990s may also uncover efforts either to reinforce or eradicate the effects of earlier decades. In addition, research aimed at quantifying the differences in educational resources and opportunities available to different racial and socioeconomic groups may aid in determining the significance and the strength of the hypothesized reciprocal correlation between educational opportunity and economic participation. Tracking the strength of this correlation or the intensity of group differences in economic resources and educational opportunities throughout the decades could reveal the national direction being taken toward equalizing access to education.

PART III

The Ointment

CHAPTER 3

Setting the Stage: 1850–1950

The histories of Glendale, Woodlawn, Sharonville, and Evandale, the four incorporated villages of the PSD, are outlined in this chapter (the remaining four districts of the PSD consolidation involved unincorporated towns and communities). The role and impact of the General Electric Company Plant upon the villages in the upper Mill Creek (Ohio) Valley are discussed here, focusing on Lincoln Heights' failure and Evandale's success in gaining this rich industrial property.

Incorporation of PSD Villages

The Princeton School District consolidation of 1953–1955 involved four districts of incorporated villages—Glendale, Woodlawn, Sharonville, and Evandale. (The boundaries of the remaining PSD districts—Springdale, Crescentville, Runyan, and Stewart—involved unincorporated communities and towns.)

Glendale

The Glendale municipality was one of the first Mill Creek Valley suburbs that sprang up along the Cincinnati, Hamilton & Dayton (CH&D) railroad lines in the mid 1800s. (Giglierano & Overmyer, 1988) The CH&D was constructed from 1849 to 1851, providing the possibility of a railway commute from the Upper Valley into the city's industrial core. Landowners and businessmen realized this possibility and laid out the residential village of Glendale. (p. 585) This new commuter suburb attracted wealthy Cincinnatians with its large lots and irregular and aesthetically pleasing street layouts. Elegant homes on winding roads just a short distance from the rail station allowed prominent businessmen to enjoy rural European-style living with an easy commute to the city or places of business. Glendale was incorporated in 1855 as a predominantly wealthy White community.

Woodlawn

Woodlawn's northern boundary neighbored Glendale and, like Glendale, was developed along the CH&D railroad line in the 1880s. (Giglierano & Overmyer, 1988) Unlike Glendale, most of Woodlawn was laid out in small lots for families of modest means. Though there were a few wealthy families living in this community, by the early 1880s most residents worked as "...teachers, farm laborers, machinists, traveling salesmen, wagonmakers, and bricklayers." (p. 590) Woodlawn also lacked the village business district that Glendale enjoyed, and the Woodlawn community tended to attract small industries. Its population was slowly growing; by 1940, the year of its incorporation, Woodlawn could boast of 1,320 residents. (p. 590) (Woodlawn's conflicts with neighboring communities, specifically Lincoln Heights, are discussed below in the section concerning the General Electric plant.)

Sharonville

At the time of PSD consolidation, the incorporated village of Sharonville shared portions of its southern and southwestern borders with the village of Evandale but was otherwise surrounded by unincorporated lands. Sharonville was settled in the 1820s by only 95 inhabitants, and by the 1840s it was still a relatively small farming community. (Giglierano & Overmyer, 1988, p. 629) The community grew steadily through the latter decades of the 1800s, reaching a population of over 400 by 1880 and increasing to approximately 600 by 1890. (p. 629) This population increase was due in part to the fact that in the 1870s, the Cleveland, Columbus, Cincinnati & Indianapolis Railroad laid lines through the community, thus attracting residents and industry. The village of Sharonville was incorporated in 1911, and by the 1920 census its population stood at 753. (Cincinnati Bureau of Governmental Research,

Inc., 1953) This northern suburb became another center for business and in-dustry, and by the 1950 census its population had reached 1,318. (p. 11) Sharonville began as an all-White settlement and even as late as the 1950 census reported only "7 negroes among its inhabitants." (p. 10) Unlike the village of Glendale, whose White inhabitants used the railway to commute to their managerial, entrepreneurial employment, Sharonville residents worked at the railway yards and shops located within their village boundaries. "In other words," states the Cincinnati Bureau of Governmental Research, Inc. (1953), "the village is remarkably homogeneous in income range, means of livelihood, and racial background. It is also self-contained in the sense that people make their living in the community in which they live, and that em-ployer and employee, place of employment and place of residence, share in the tax burdens growing out of the needs of their Village and of their school." (p. 11) Protecting this "homogeneity" was a factor in the conflicts surrounding the PDS consolidation of the 1950s.

Evandale
(The history of Evandale is outlined in the following section because of its obvious links to what became the General Electric Company Plant of Evan-dale and the fact that their histories are intertwined.)

The General Electric Company Plant: Vying for Industrial Properties

The General Electric Company plant was important to several communities in the Upper Mill Creek Valley because it would provide a considerable tax base to the community that could incorporate or annex those properties. Ef-forts to incorporate those valuable properties predate the presence of the General Electric Company plant or its predecessor, the Wright Aeronautical Plant.

What is now known as the General Electric Company Aircraft Engine Group's Evandale Plant resides on a tract of land that until 1940 was occu-pied "...by farms and the homes of some lower-income black families in a subdivision called Valley View." (Giglierano & Overmyer, 1988 p. 576) Valley View was one of several Black subdivisions formed as a result of mi-gration from the overcrowded industrial center of the 1920s. Valley View and other adjacent Black subdivisions sought to unify in efforts to obtain basic public services and resources that were lacking. Taylor (1979) tells of the frustrations that residents of these inferior dwellings and neighborhoods encountered when attempting to secure such basics as water, sewage and garbage disposal, roads, and electricity from the city, county, or township leaders. This frustration and failure served to unite, to some degree, the ten separate subdivisions that, with the exception of Valley View, would come to make up the village of Lincoln Heights. The need to come together for common goals was the first step toward incorporating the Black neighborhoods and subdivisions. It would also be the beginning or, for some, the acceleration of conflicts with neighboring White communities.

Lincoln Heights' Struggle to Incorporate

During this time in Cincinnati history, from 1920 to 1940, it was the responsibility of the townships in which unincorporated communities were located and the city commissioners to provide for community development and improvement. However, the requests and concerns of Black residents were generally ignored or given a very low priority. For this reason, a number of leaders in these adjacent subdivisions began making efforts to incorporate into a unified, autonomous, self-sufficient, and self-governing entity. Not all residents agreed that incorporation was the proper step to take. Many believed that incorporation would lead to higher taxes, stringent building and zoning codes that they could not adhere to, and the ultimate loss of property and homes. Therefore, the move to incorporate the Black subdivisions in the Upper Mill Creek Valley was not without internal struggle while, at the same time, those who led the charge for incorporation also faced difficulties with external forces. Most of the external problems concerned conflicts over real or potential industrial properties that the Black residents were occupying and industrial lands that lay adjacent to the subdivisions, both of which the Black leaders considered part of the incorporation efforts. As Taylor (1979) observes: "In essence, the black settlement lay in the heart of the enormously rich industrial region of northern Hamilton County." (p. 293)

Those supporting incorporation were looking to the taxes gained from current and future industries to finance the growth of their village. "Although there were only a handful of factories located in the upper Mill Creek Valley in the late 1930s," explains Taylor (1979), "the area was projected to become a giant industrial park, filled with hundreds of industrial and commercial concerns valued in the billions of dollars." (p. 294) So despite the internal struggles and opposing opinions "...[t]hose who favored continued unity with the township trustees were temporarily silenced and in the fall of 1936, the residents voted to support the consolidation of the subdivisions and the fight for self government." (p. 301) There was a great deal of work involved in the move to unite these separate subdivisions into a village, but "[a]fter seven years of careful planning and preparation, the residents were ready to file for incorporation." (p. 306)

In the meantime, however, the first significant external conflict occurred between the Black subdivisions and the Woodlawn community. In May of 1940, Woodlawn petitioned the county commissioners to incorporate its village, claiming a considerable portion of the same land specified in the Lincoln Heights petition. Both petitions were subsequently rejected by the commissioners, and the parties were instructed to settle their own boundary disputes. Rather than engage in a lengthy legal battle, Lincoln Heights leaders relinquished claims to the residential property in question in addition to some of the industrial land located in the Valley View subdivision. They believed that after giving up the controversial lands, the Lincoln Heights village would still have "enough industrial and commercial property to structure a sound economic base." (p. 312)

Incorporation would still not be an easily won battle. Opposition continued from within the subdivisions, but, more importantly, Woodlawn would prove to be only one of the external forces against incorporation, particularly if incorporation included the remaining industrial lands in the Valley View subdivision. In fact, Taylor (1979) contends that "The Defense Corporation and the Wright Aeronautical Corporation were the most powerful opponents of the incorporation of Lincoln Heights to emerge." (p. 327) Land adjacent to the Valley View subdivision was purchased by the Defense Corporation and leased to the Wright Aeronautical Company. Taylor goes on to explain the plans that motivated these acquisitions:

> The Defense Corporation was also in the process of obtaining most of the land in the Valley View Subdivision. Wright Aeronautical planned to construct a massive airplane factory on this site....When completed, it would be the largest plant of its kind in the United States, and the leading employer in Cincinnati and Hamilton County. (p. 328)

In 1942 the Wright plant filed an objection to the Lincoln Heights incorporation with the county commissioners. Taylor's analysis states that Wright
Aeronautical, like other businesses and industries, was not interested in paying high taxes in order to support communities. Newspaper articles reflecting
back on these events also underscore Wright's resistance to Lincoln Heights'
incorporation efforts:

> Representing Wright, the Cincinnati law firm of Frost and Jacobs wrote the county
> commissioners that Lincoln Heights' incorporation of Valley View "would make
> the limits of the village unreasonably large." The attorneys argued that...it would be
> "unjust or inequitable" to grant Valley View to Lincoln Heights. (Lincoln Heights
> Grows, 1970, 13)

After more delays, the leaders for incorporation came to believe that their
efforts would not go forward unless they relinquished the Valley View Subdivision. This belief was later expressed in a newspaper article reflecting on
the incorporation of Lincoln Heights:

> By 1944, the "heat from Wright was unbearable," Fulton, agent for the incorpora-
> tions, said, "It was hinted that if the (Valley View) area were excluded there would
> be a more favorable climate for Lincoln Heights incorporation. The area sought to
> be incorporated then was whittled down to where it was unofficially stated this di-
> minished area would be granted." (Lincoln Heights Grows, 1970, 13)

Though internal struggles and delays continued, brought on by subdivision
residents opposed to consolidation, the Board of County Commissioners approved the incorporation of Lincoln Heights without the valuable property.
(Taylor, 1979) Robinson (1970a) notes:

> The commissioners said federal authorities responsible for building the Wright plant
> preferred that it remain in unincorporated territory until it was disposed of. In 1946,
> after deleting the industrial portion of the territory sought, the commissioners
> granted incorporation to a total land area of 0.804 square miles. (p. 1)

Though the quest for consolidation of the Black Upper Mill Creek Valley subdivisions began before the Defense Corporation purchased land adjacent to Valley View or purchased the subdivision itself, the Wright
Aeronautical Plant buildings were completed long before Lincoln Heights
became an incorporated village. According to Giglierano and Overmyer
(1988), "The land was quickly acquired, the residents were moved—

apparently most of the black families went to nearby Lincoln Heights—and by June 1941, the massive complex was completed." (p. 576)

Evandale Gains the Prize

Until its closing in 1945, the Wright plant produced aircraft engines for the war effort. In 1948 the General Electric Company leased a portion of the plant and began producing jet engines. Still residing on unincorporated land, surrounding villages hoped to annex this valuable industrial property. (Giglierano & Overmyer, 1988, p. 575) However, with a population of only 360, "…a new municipality, Evandale, was incorporated in 1950. Evandale claimed the cluster of defense plants as a part of its territory and a court decision the following year approved that claim, to the dismay of residents and officials of Lincoln Heights, Reading, and Lockland." (p. 577) Perhaps none were more dismayed than the citizens of Lincoln Heights. The mayor of Lincoln Heights in an interview with a Black newspaper clearly articulated his disappointment and frustration, stating, "we see no reason why a handful of people such as live in Evandale should be permitted to incorporate merely to grab what rightfully belongs to our community." (Former Wright, 1950/1979, p. 1) Mayor Shivers went on to outline Lincoln Heights' entitlement to the property, its extreme need of the tax income to provide services for its people, and the community's intention to file an injunction against Evandale's incorporation:

> In our petition for our proposed annexation, we are asking for what rightfully belongs to us. We are asking for a natural boundary. The petition is asking for what was originally planned for our boundary lines. We were asked to withdraw from the Wright property area because the Government didn't want it incorporated or annexed. Being patriotic, we complied. We have been refused this territory twice for the reason stated above…we are hoping for favorable action and justice. We are asking for that which is equitable—for what is ethical and just for Lincoln Heights. (p. 1)

However, incorporation was granted to Evandale, which included the disputed properties. Evandale's incorporation supplied the final wall on Lincoln

Heights' eastern boundary that would landlock the Black village, preventing its further expansion and economic development. If Lincoln Heights had been granted incorporation to include the properties in their original petition, the municipality's economic situation would have been quite different by the time of the 1970 school district merger. "The area on the original petition for incorporation included present Lincoln Heights plus chunks of what now are Evendale and Woodlawn....If Lincoln Heights encompassed those boundary lines today, its area would be more than twice its present size and its tax base would be fed by General Electric, the Ford Motor Company and the Brunswick Corporation among others." ("Too Little", 1970, p. 11)

Figure 3 shows the properties included in Lincoln Heights' original petition but eliminated when the village was finally incorporated. The map was printed in 1974 and depicts the situation after more industries had moved into the area; nevertheless, the broken line indicates the extent of Lincoln Heights' loss of valuable land in its 1946 incorporation. (Lincoln Heights: Now a Chance, 1974) Evendale's economic situation, on the other hand, would simply improve as the General Electric plant grew through the 1950s and 1960s to become, by the 1970s and 1980s, "the largest single employer in Greater Cincinnati." (Giglierano & Overmyer, 1988, p. 577) "The new Village of Evendale," explains Giglierano and Overmyer, "...had the best industrial tax base of any village in the county, and the number of manufacturers in Evendale continued to increase as more firms took advantage of the area's large building sites and its proximity to the I-75 Expressway." (p. 575)

The Reed and Reed (1953) report points to the incorporation of Lincoln Heights and Evendale as blatant examples of the inequalities in the distribution of resources manifested in metropolitan Cincinnati. (p.16) Speaking of Evendale's incorporation, they state, "...there is no equity in a system which permits one local entity, *deliberately and artificially created*, to base its village taxes on $44,000 of assessed valuation per capita while 19 others in Hamilton County base theirs on less than $2,000." (emphasis added; p. 20) The inequity is even more pronounced when specifically comparing Evendale's economic status to Lincoln Heights' with the latter having a 1950 assessed valuation of $3,261,000, or a $590 per capita valuation for its 5,531 residents. (pp. 20–21) This situation led Reed and Reed (1953) to conclude, "There is something egregiously wrong with a system of metropolitan government in which an Evendale and a Lincoln Heights can exist side by side." (p. 21)

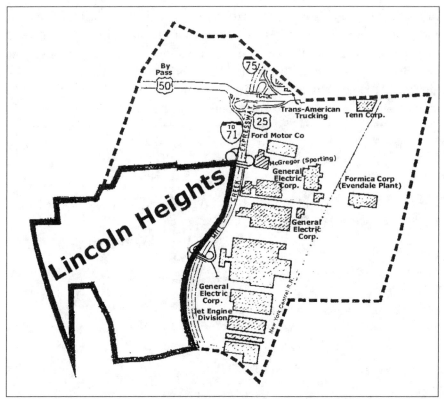

Figure 3. Valuable Property Lost to Lincoln Heights.
The solid line represents Lincoln Heights village boundaries. The dotted line represents the industrial area eliminated when Lincoln Heights incorporated in 1946. Composite created from map data in "Lincoln Heights: Now a Chance to Overcome Most Difficulties of the Past," *The Cincinnati Enquirer*, 16 September 1974, p. 19.

These economic links will be important later when examining the Lincoln Heights situation in the 1950s through 1970s and its relationship to villages within the Princeton district during that time period. For example, Princeton School District's 1957 transfer of $6.5 million of tax valuation of the General Electric Company Plant in Evandale for the building of a new high school in Lincoln Heights can be interpreted quite differently when viewed in isolation in contrast to being viewed in light of the history of Lincoln Heights' struggle and failure to secure these industrial lands that were originally inhabited by Black residents. Knowing that Lincoln Heights relinquished the property on which the General Electric plant now stands and witnessed its incorporation into the extremely small White municipality of

Evandale a few years later may make the transfer of tax valuation from the same property for the purposes of building an all-Black high school seem less of a benevolent gift than when viewed without knowledge of these past events and circumstances. This economic link also resurfaces when the Lincoln Heights District is merged with the Princeton School district in 1970 and will be addressed again in later chapters.

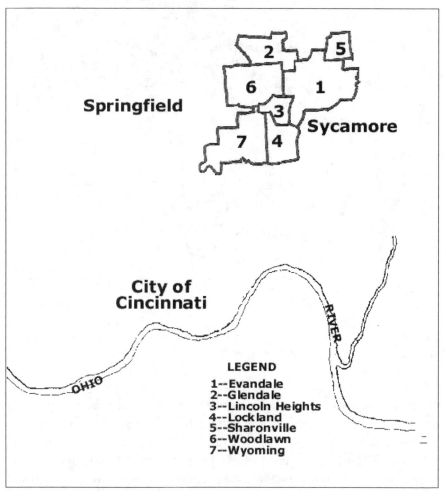

Figure 4. Incorporated Areas in Northern Hamilton County.
Composite created from map data in D. D. Reed and T. H. Reed, *The Cincinnati Area Must Solve Its Metropolitan Problems* (Cincinnati Dunie Printing Co., 1953), p. 45.

CHAPTER 4

Creating and Consolidating Districts: 1946–1955

In this chapter, the histories of the eight school districts of the PSD are out-lined (Evandale, Glendale, Woodlawn, Sharonville, Springdale, Crescent-ville, Stewart, and Runyan). The unrest in these communities surrounding pro- and anti-consolidation arguments is also discussed. The creation of LHSD is revisited and its exclusion from PSD analyzed.

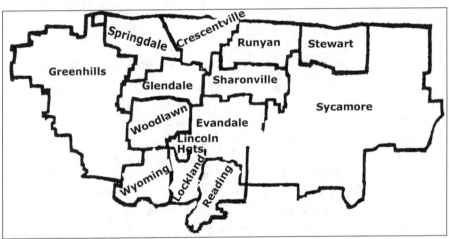

Figure 5. Hamilton County School Districts in the Upper Mill Creek Valley.
Composite created from map data in "Schools Big Hurdle in Annexation Path," *The Cincin-nati Enquirer*, 28 October 1951, p. 37.

In comparing Figure 4 and Figure 5, it is apparent that school district lines seldom approximate the boundaries of incorporated villages. (also see Reed & Reed, 1953, p. 45; Schools Big Hurdle, 1951, p. 37) More often than not, an individual school district will overlap into the properties of adjoining incorporated villages and may also include adjacent unincorporated lands. For example, even after Evandale was incorporated, the Evandale School District contained most of its village along with parts of three adjacent dis-tricts, Lockland, Sharonville, and Sycamore districts. (Reed & Reed, 1953, p.

13) This fact made the school situation in Greater Cincinnati and Hamilton County very complex in that only four of its forty districts had boundaries that coincided with city or village lines. (p. 13) As a result, economic and social concerns arose as districts struggled to support the education of "the horde of children that poured into the suburbs by the outward movement of population." (p. 12) As outlined in the previous chapter, not all incorporated villages and cities were created equal either economically or in land area. The consolidation of districts and, in one case, the creation of a district were direct outgrowths of these inequities and the economic and social issues of the time.

Another Conflict: Creating the Lincoln Heights School District

The historical problems of Lincoln Heights led naturally to similar problems for the schools. Once the boundaries were established for the municipality, the die was cast for education. And the ensuing 20 years have recorded setbacks and broken dreams. (City Problems, 1970, p. 10)

At this point it is important to note the events that were taking place between the villages of Woodlawn and Lincoln Heights and the Hamilton County Board of Education between 1949 and 1953—from the initial recommendation for redistricting and consolidation to the passing of the consolidation resolution by the county board. Lincoln Heights' exclusion is as much a part of PSD's history as is Woodlawn's inclusion. At the same time that the county board redefined the Woodlawn district, it also created the new Lincoln Heights School District. (see chapter 2) Woodlawn would remain a part of the county system whereas "...the municipality of Lincoln Heights, with its low valuation, is the area which was expected to become a city school district and therefore no longer a concern of the county school board." (Harris & Erickson, 1951, p. 66)

Harris and Erickson go on to explain, "There are indications here that the white minority pulled out taking with them the bulk of the wealth, in order to become a majority in the new Woodlawn district." (p. 67)

Having wrested itself from Lincoln Heights and yet remaining a part of the county system, Woodlawn was free to become a part of the new consolidation. One problem with the 1950 board decision was that even after Woodlawn redefined its district to exclude Lincoln Heights' properties, the neighboring Lockland and Evandale districts still overlapped into Lincoln Heights. Therefore Lincoln Heights should not have been designated as having a school district coinciding with its corporation lines because of the remaining overlapping districts. (see chapter 2) Creating the Lincoln Heights district thereby affected the racial and economic compositions of previously overlapping districts. Evandale, in particular, no longer included any Lincoln Heights property or therefore any Black Lincoln Heights students. Evandale was, in fact, listed in the initial 1949 proposal the prior year.

Once Lincoln Heights attained city status after the 1950 census, Ohio law required that the school district become a city district. (City Problems, 1970) This meant the new LHSD would need to be financially independent and no longer able to benefit from the county's resources and services. *The Cincinnati Enquirer* later reported:

> County Supt. John Wilson said there was an attempt at that time to get a bill passed in the state legislature so that Lincoln Heights could remain a local district under jurisdiction of the county board. He said Lincoln Heights wanted to be a local district in order to get better services for its children. (City Problems, 1970, p. 10)

This desire is verified in the Lincoln Heights board minutes:

> The clerk then stated that he had talked with Superintendent Crouch and Asst. Superintendent Wilson and that they suggested that our board write the county board a letter if we desired to remain under county supervision. (Lincoln Heights School Board Meeting Minutes, 1951, February 7)

The Hamilton County Board minutes reflect that it received said correspondence from the Lincoln Heights Board:

> A communication was received from the Board of Education of the Lincoln Heights Local School District, stating that Board wishes to remain under the supervision of the Hamilton County Board of Education. (Hamilton County Board of Education Meeting Minutes, 1951, March 13)

The wishes of the Lincoln Heights Board were not granted until 1961 when a bill was passed in the Ohio legislature that allowed cities to maintain local districts under county jurisdiction. At that time "Lincoln Heights then changed from its city district status back to local district status." (City Problems, 1970, p. 10)

Consolidation in the Upper Valley: The Princeton School District

A brief look at the economic and racial/ethnic makeups of the eight districts and their histories will illuminate not only the initial PSD consolidation struggles but also the subsequent LHSD/PSD merger 15 years later.

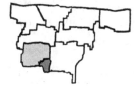

Woodlawn

By the 1950s, at the time of the PSD consolidation, 35% of Woodlawn's residents were Black. Prior to 1950, Woodlawn maintained two elementary schools, one of which was located in the Lincoln Heights community, Woodlawn South, and had an all-Black student enrollment. The elementary school within Woodlawn's village boundaries was named Woodlawn North and accommodated the children residing in the village. The combined enrollment of the two schools was 1,272 students in grades one through eight and 108 pupils in kindergarten. (Harris & Erickson, 1952)

The Woodlawn valuation per pupil for that year was $2,802. Because the Hamilton County Board of Education redefined Woodlawn's school district to coincide with its city lines, the Woodlawn School District was only responsible for the Black children who resided within its village boundaries. Moreover, after the redefinition of the Woodlawn School District, Woodlawn South became Lincoln Heights Elementary, and per-pupil valuation for the Woodlawn School District rose to $8,801. (p. 11) This move by the Hamilton County Board of Education, at the urging of Woodlawn, left the newly created Lincoln Heights School District with a low valuation of $1,544 per child. (p. 11)

It should be noted that even after Woodlawn redefined its district lines, making it responsible only for the Black students residing there, some White families residing near the western border of the village sent their elementary-school-age children, on a tuition basis, to the large, neighboring, practically all White Greenhills School District. (Cincinnati Bureau of Governmental Research, Inc., 1953, p. 11)

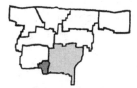

Evandale

After Evandale's incorporation in 1950, the growth of the village was carefully controlled. In 1953, a plan was developed to restrict both commercial and residential development. (Giglierano & Overmyer, 1988) Though Evandale was industrially rich from the beginning and though companies such as Ford Motor Company and Formica joined the ranks with General Electric, the controlled growth plan provided room for industrial expansion as late as 20 to 30 years after its incorporation. (p. 575) Despite the limits on corporate growth, by 1960 the restriction on residential development allowed Evandale to employ in its factories approximately 75,000 workers while only housing approximately 1,200. (p. 275)

In the same year that this growth plan was outlined by the village officials, the County Board of Education approved the school consolidation plan that included Evandale. Evandale built an elementary school in 1932, and by 1950, when the Hamilton County Board of Education distributed its plan for consolidation, this school employed two teachers and enrolled only 69 students in grades one through three. (Hamilton County Board of Education, 1950, p. 16) According to the 1949 tax valuation of $5,914,600, Evandale could boast of a per-pupil ratio of $85,000. (p. 10) By 1952 Evandale's assessed valuation had increased to $14,120,260 while its student enrollment had risen to a mere 78. These changes afforded Evandale a per-pupil valuation ratio of $181,028. (Reed & Reed, 1953) This figure is contrasted against the $2,282 of assessed valuation that Lincoln Heights had available in that same year for each of its kindergarten through eighth grade pupils. (p. 14)

Though the Evandale school district overlapped into the incorporated village of Lincoln Heights prior to 1950, the county's creation of the Lincoln Heights School District that coincided with its own boundaries simultaneously and by default removed the Lincoln Heights properties from the Evandale School District. As a result, even if integrated schooling were permitted in Evandale prior to 1950, it was virtually impossible after the neighboring Black students were removed from the district and only White students resided in the Evandale village. The restrictions on residential construction instilled a few years later likely prevented Blacks in neighboring Lincoln Heights from spilling over into Evandale.

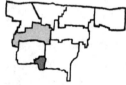

Glendale

Glendale was incorporated in 1855 and began as a predominantly wealthy White community that even as late as the 1980s had fewer than 20% Black inhabitants. This again is compared to neighboring Woodlawn's growth from 35% Black in the 1950s to 80% in the 1980s. Of course Lincoln Heights, its neighbor to the south, remained nearly 100% Black during those years. Until its consolidation within the PDS in the 1950s, Glendale maintained segregated schooling for the Black elementary school pupils that resided in its district. The original school building that accommodated its White pupils was constructed in 1901 with a large addition erected in 1933. (Hamilton County Board of Education, 1950, p. 14) In 1950, the main school building accommodated 215 elementary students, kindergarten through eighth grade, and 91 high school students, grades nine through twelve. The building employed 18 teachers, a pupil/teacher ratio of 17/1. (p. 14)

The school for "Negro" children was located only approximately one mile from the main building. In 1950, this building accommodated 92 pupils, kindergarten through eighth grade, and employed four teachers, yielding a pupil/teacher ratio of 23/1. (p. 14) This building had been a residence before its conversion into a schoolhouse. It was quite small in comparison to the main building and lacked many of the facilities enjoyed by students accommodated in the latter. Obviously Glendale maintained segregated elementary

schools through the mid 1950s because of its desire to do so. The close proximity of the two schools rules out maintenance of the parallel systems for the
purpose of keeping schools close to respective neighborhoods. Neither was a
lack of space in the main building an issue. Concerning the main Glendale
school building, the 1950 Hamilton County consolidation plan reports,
"[t]his is an excellent school plant....Many more pupils could be accommodated than are now enrolled." (p. 14) These separate systems were maintained at the same time that Glendale managed to keep low percentages of
Black residents.

The assessed valuations for Glendale, based on the 1949 tax year, was
$4,083,980. (p. 10) For the combined student bodies in its two buildings,
398, this high total valuation yielded an equally high per-pupil valuation of
$10,261.

Sharonville

As noted in the previous chapter concerning its incorporation, Sharonville
was a predominately White, self-contained, "homogeneous" community, reporting only seven African Americans in the 1950 census. (Cincinnati Bureau of Governmental Research, Inc., 1953) The Sharonville School District
bordered three of the school districts involved in the PSD consolidation—
Glendale, Crescentville, and Runyan. In years prior to the PSD consolidation
proposal, Sharonville schools accepted many children from other districts,
primarily Runyan and Stewart districts, because Sharonville accommodated
grade levels absent in the others. Perhaps the racial and ethnic makeups of
the Runyan and Stewart communities failed to threaten the "homogeneity" of
Sharonville, for the latter preferred a consolidation limited to a union with
the former two districts. (p. 11)

Sharonville's school building was constructed in 1926 with several additions erected in later years. It housed both elementary and high school students. (Hamilton County Board of Education, 1950) In 1950, 329 students
were enrolled in kindergarten through eighth grade and 154 students in
grades nine through twelve. (p. 15) Sharonville's assessed valuation of

$7,648,850 and total student enrollment of 483 produced a per-pupil valuation of $15,836. (p. 10) The elementary school employed eleven teachers, which yielded a 29/1 pupil/teacher ratio, and the high school employed seven teachers, which produced a pupil/teacher ratio of 22/1. (p. 15)

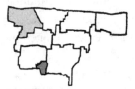

Springdale

Springdale was not an incorporated village at the time of the PSD consolidation. (It was incorporated in 1959 so it was an independent municipality at the time of the PSD/Lincoln Heights merger of 1970.) Springdale lies on the northwest border of the village of Glendale and extends up to the county line. The town was inhabited as early as 1792 and by 1821 had approximately 220 inhabitants. (Giglierano & Overmyer, 1988) When the Cincinnati, Hamilton & Dayton Railroad laid tracks through Glendale, attracting residents and businesses to that neighboring village to the south, Springdale's population slowed considerably. However, after World War II, as industry in the Upper Mill Creek Valley increased, Springdale began to enjoy growth in its populace. (p. 630) Springdale, reportedly, was also attracting new families because of its school building and school program. (Cincinnati Bureau of Governmental Research, Inc., 1953) Most of the homes were inexpensive and modest relative to those in other communities such as Glendale, while Springdale's tax duplicate consisted largely of this residential property along with the tax duplicate from the railway lines. Though Springdale would grow considerably in the 20 years following the PSD consolidation, maintaining its school budget and finances was a delicate balance. (p. 13)

Springdale residents were described as "homogeneous" (p. 13), indicating its lack of racial diversity or, more specifically, its lack of a Black population. The one elementary school in Springdale during the time of the consolidation was built in 1927. The 1949 enrollment of 180 students in grades one through eight, with its six teachers, produced a 30/1 pupil/teacher ratio. (Hamilton County Board of Education, 1950, p. 16) Based on the 1949 tax year, Springdale's assessed valuation was $1,675,290 and its per-pupil valuation was $9,307. (p. 10)

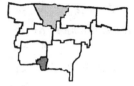

Crescentville

The Crescentville School District bordered four of the eight districts involved in the PSD consolidation, with Springdale on the western border, Glendale southern, and Sharonville and Runyan eastern. Crescentville extends north to the county line. The Crescentville community was a rural community with little industry to aid in the support of its school system. Though by the early 1950s the Crescentville School District had increased its tax duplicates to adequately handle its school budget, any significant increases in school enrollment concomitant with increases in cost per pupil would easily threaten the fiscal balance. (Cincinnati Bureau of Governmental Research, Inc., 1953, p. 13)

Crescentville's two-room elementary school was built in 1904. The 1950 Hamilton County Board of Education's plan for consolidation reported an enrollment of 49 pupils in grades one through eight. (Hamilton County Board of Education, 1950, p. 16) With two teachers employed, the pupil/teacher ratio was 24/1. Crescentville's assessed valuation, based on the 1949 tax year, was $711,590; therefore its per-pupil valuation was $14,522.

Runyan

The Runyan School District lies north of Sharonville and between the eastern border of the Crescentville School District and the western border of the Stewart School District. Runyan had a good financial status at the time of the PSD consolidation and could not only boast of a debt-free school building but also had one of the lowest tax rates in the country. (Cincinnati Bureau of Governmental Research, Inc., 1953) Runyan owed its financial status to several factors. During its transition from a rural to an urban area, the federal government purchased much of the farmland, converting taxable land into tax-exempt holdings. In addition, in the years following there was an overall growth in industry, which subsequently increased the tax duplicates for the district. These two factors combined with the fact that Runyan experienced no significant increases in school-age children left the district in good financial stead by the early 1950s. (p. 12)

Runyan's elementary school building was erected in 1929 and at the time of consolidation had no indoor plumbing. Grades one through eight accommodated 40 students and two teachers, providing a pupil/teacher ratio of 20/1. (Hamilton County Board of Education, 1950, p. 17) Based on the 1949 tax year, Runyan reported an assessed valuation of $2,623,290 and, therefore, a per-pupil assessed valuation of $65,582. Runyan sent its high school students to Sharonville; therefore, this per-pupil calculation does not take into account the support of high school students that lived in the Runyan district but attended school in Sharonville.

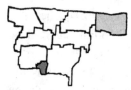

Stewart

The Stewart School District was by far the poorest of the eight districts in the PSD consolidation and was indeed suffering financial distress. The inexpensive homes that comprised the community did not supply adequate tax duplicates to support the education of the number of children housed there. Unlike its neighboring Runyan School District, Stewart lacked significant industry and tax-exempt lands to relieve its financial crisis. In fact, if Stewart were rescued through consolidation with wealthier districts, the consolidation plan would have to include the Runyan School District. Consolidation rules demanded that the districts involved share common borders. (Hamilton County Board of Education, 1950, p. 4) The Stewart School District bordered the Runyan School District to the west and extended north to the county line. Because its southern and eastern borders were shared with the large Sycamore District, Stewart's only other option to a consolidation involving Runyan would be annexation to the Sycamore District. (Figure 5) The Stewart School District had an ongoing relationship with the Sharonville School District in that many children attended the Sharonville schools. However, since

Stewart shared no borders with Sharonville, it could only be included in a consolidation involving Sharonville if Runyan were also included.

The school building that accommodated Stewart's elementary students was built in 1879 and, at the time of consolidation, lacked indoor plumbing. In 1950, 80 pupils were enrolled in grades one through four and the Stewart school employed two teachers. (Hamilton County Board of Education, 1950, p. 17) The pupil/teacher ratio was 40/1, and, calculated from an assessed valuation of $438,430, the per-pupil valuation was $5,480. Students in grades five through twelve attended Sharonville schools. This per-pupil valuation does not include the support of Sharonville students.

Unrest in PSD Communities

The consolidation of the eight Upper Valley communities and local districts into PSD was the result of a 1949 study, commissioned by the county board of education, of the local districts in Hamilton County. A plan for redistricting was to be submitted at the conclusion of the study. (Luke, 1981a) Initially the study recommended seven districts for consolidation. Woodlawn was latter added to the consolidation resolution, but "Lincoln Heights asked to be excluded." (p. 5)

Common to both the 1950 decision by the county board to create or redefine the Lincoln Heights and Woodlawn districts and the 1953 decision to create the consolidated Princeton district is the questionable legality of the decisions. Though the 1950 Lincoln Heights/Woodlawn decision was never formally questioned, the Hamilton County Board of Education's 1953 decision to create the new consolidated PSD found its way in the Court of Common Pleas, the Court of Appeals, and the Ohio State Supreme Court. One question was "...whether the county board had exceeded its rights in passing the consolidation resolution." (Luke, 1981a, p. 5) However, in 1955 the State Supreme Court allowed the decision for the new consolidated PSD to stand. It is then apparent that the PSD consolidation was not without conflicts within and among the individual districts. These pro- and anti-consolidation factions led to the Hamilton County Board of Education's 1953 decision finding its way into the courts.

Pro-Consolidation Arguments

District consolidation was viewed by many as a solution to the school problems of the city and county. Just as villages and cities were incorporated with
extreme differences in geographic area and residential and industrial taxable
wealth, so were the school districts that emerged in Hamilton County. There
were also vast differences in the grade levels offered by the districts, most
importantly, as to whether the districts offered high school education or had
to send their children out of the district. Some districts had large enrollments
whereas others were so small as to make "…it impossible to provide in them
a well rounded system of education except at prohibitive expense." (Reed &
Reed, 1953, p. 14) There were also extreme variations in the tax valuations
of the school districts, which further complicated the situation. Educators
reacting to reports of uneconomic and ineffectual schooling looked at school
district consolidation as a possible remedy. In this vein, the state department
of education recommended consolidation of most of the local districts in
Hamilton County. The arguments for consolidation thereby centered around
eliminating inequalities in resources and educational opportunities among the
neighboring districts.

The Hamilton County Board of Education lists the following advantages
of district consolidation:

1. A larger district has a greater tax duplicate, which, in turn, permits the board of
   education to have available funds to finance a more thorough program of education.
2. A district with strong financial resources pays good salaries, and good salaries
   attract and hold good teachers.
3. School districts with adequate operating funds are in a position to buy the kinds
   of material needed to give the boys and girls of the Hamilton County School
   District what they deserve.
4. Larger schools permit one teacher per grade on the elementary level—a distinct
   advantage in instruction.
5. Larger tax duplicates permit more building.
   (Hamilton County Board of Education, 1950, p. 6)

Harris and Erickson (1952) detailed the consolidation movement in Ohio
schools. They also emphasized the fact that consolidation was seen as a solution to poorly organized schools within the state, schools' inefficient use of
facilities, and their failure to met minimum standards set forth by the state.
Ohio's minimum standards for schools were as follows:

1. The *minimum* enrollment in an elementary school of grades 1-6 shall be 180 with at least one teacher per grade; for an elementary school of grades 1–8, 240 pupils with at least eight teachers.
2. The minimum enrollment for a six-year secondary school shall be 300, with at least twelve teachers. The minimum enrollment for a four-year secondary school shall be 225. For economical provision of services an enrollment of 300–600 is highly recommended.
    (Harris & Erickson, 1952, p. 3)

The schools in the eight districts described in the previous section clearly failed to meet Ohio's minimum standards. Proponents of consolidation believed that underattended schools and schools with too few teachers would benefit from joining with schools in neighboring districts. Table 1 uses data from the Hamilton County Board of Education (1950) report to demonstrate whether the seven districts (Woodlawn was not included in the plan at this time) met the minimum standards concerning student enrollments and the number of employed teachers. First of all, it should be noted that only two of the districts, Sharonville and Glendale, offered high school programs. Secondly, based upon 1949/50 data, all but one of the districts' elementary schools, Sharonville's elementary school, failed to meet Ohio's minimum standards, reporting low enrollments and a low number of employed teachers. Proponents of consolidation used these data to demonstrate that even the wealthy districts were unable to provide a rich and broad, or even adequate, education for their children. In 1952, Harris and Erickson reported:

> Often "rich school districts," such as Evandale with its $104,000 per-pupil valuation not only fail to provide any or adequate high schools for their pupils, but also fail to provide proper educational organization or services for their elementary pupils as well. The inclusion of such districts in consolidation in order to raise the tax duplicate of the new district as a whole and to provide proper enrollment in all schools, would seem in line with sound educational thought. (p. 8)

Harris and Erickson articulated the advantages set forth by consolidation proponents as follows:

1. Better instruction through proper deployment of teachers and pupils.
2. Greater efficiency of operation through centralized administration of maintenance and janitorial services, more efficient bus routes, central purchasing, etc.
3. Financing advantages through broader tax valuations.
4. Social advantages from mixing students from various backgrounds. (p. 4)

Table 1: Do Eight District Schools Meet Ohio's Minimum Standards? Data from Hamilton County Board of Education, (1950).

District School(s)	Gr. 1–6 180/6*	Gr. 1–8 240/8*	Gr. 7–12 300/12*	Gr. 9–12 225/?*
Woodlawn				
Evandale	No (Gr.1–3 69/3)	--	--	--
Glendale				
Main	--	Yes (215)	--	No (91)
"Negro"	--	No (92/4)	--	--
Sharonville		Yes (329/11)	--	No (154/7)
Springdale	--	No (180/6)	--	--
Crescentville	--	No (49/2)	--	--
Runyan	--	No (40/2)	--	--
Stewart	No (Gr. 1–4 80/2)	--	--	--

*Minimum standard enrollments/teachers for schools with these grade levels

Those who advocated the PDS consolidation reiterated the advantages reported by the Hamilton County Board of Education and in the document of Harris and Erickson when advancing their arguments. As detailed above, the districts involved differed in their abilities to build and maintain physical plants, offer educational programs, maintain low pupil/teacher ratios, and employ highly qualified teachers. In essence supporters presented consolidation as cost effective and argued that it would benefit all involved.

Anti-Consolidation Arguments

Harris and Erickson (1952) also listed the disadvantages of consolidation that were generally put forward by those opposed to the joining of districts as follows:

1. Education should be close to the people; larger districts tend to remove a certain intimacy and control now associated with our schools.
2. If consolidation is badly planned, it can disrupt the existing education provided.
3. Some children will have to travel farther to school. (p. 4)

Concerns over loss of control over the schools in the respective communities and concerns over potential tax increases, though the latter were not listed by Harris and Erickson as disadvantages, were certainly the most verbalized causes of the discord that resulted from the eight-district PDS consolidation plan. In such a consolidation, the local school districts do indeed loose all control for they are subsequently disbanded. The board of education for the new consolidated district is then established, and its charter members are appointed by the County Board of Education. (Hamilton County Board of Education, 1950, p. 5) Though the successors to the consolidated board of education are then elected to their positions, initially the citizens in the communities involved have no input to or control of this new board. Moreover, communities permanently lose significant control over teacher hiring, curricula, and most other aspects of their neighborhood schools. Concerns over increased tax burdens that would potentially result from consolidation of districts, tended to come more from the communities that were relatively wealthy. For example, though the Glendale Local Board of Education actually proposed the original seven-district consolidation (which did not include Woodlawn), a very vocal anti-consolidation group emerged from this wealthy community. According to Reed and Reed (1953) this was a common reaction and obstacle, making consolidation and grouping of neighboring districts difficult. They point out, "... the districts with relatively large tax values naturally shy away from combination with poor districts, involving the loss of their favorable financial position and certain increases in taxes for schools." (p. 14)

The less-vocalized but more implied objections to consolidation may have given rise to the most passionately felt and powerful anti-consolidation sentiments. These objections centered on racist or classist feelings that are often not overtly spoken or documented. Reed and Reed (1953) concur that this second difficulty in consolidating neighboring districts "...is based on racial and social distinctions of which little is said publicly." (p. 14) These covert objections are sometimes revealed inadvertently, for example, in the nature of statements made in the propaganda literature. One open letter to the community read "The rich get richer and the poor have more children." On the surface this may seem to be only about money but it is really about the stereotypical characteristics of those who do not have money and a resistance to a consolidation plan that would integrate these children into their schools. A government report predicted such objections or problems but presented them as benign, natural concerns communities had over maintaining their "homogeneity."

Because people like to flock with their own kind, and because nothing is ever static in an area for long, small communities come to exist for a time side by side, each endeavoring to protect its own particular brand of homogeneity against encroach-

ment by its neighbors....Glendale, it is true, has managed to control its own situation for almost a century....Sharonville, similarly, has protected its own homogeneity—not without internal dissentions, it is true—within the narrow limits of its
Village boundaries. (Cincinnati Bureau of Governmental Research, Inc., 1953, p.
13)

If Sharonville's school board shared these concerns for homogeneity, it obviously did not feel that it would be jeopardized in a consolidation with Runyan and Stewart school districts. A representative from Sharonville objected
to the proposed eight-district consolidation and proposed the alternate three-
district consolidation with Runyan and Stewart. Perhaps their unspoken concerns had more to do with racial makeups of the other communities rather
than the economic makeup of the financially distressed Stewart School District. It should be pointed out that the eight consolidated districts would in-
herit each others' Black population and that districts, such as Glendale,
which had, up to that time, maintained segregated schooling for its small
Black population would be forced to integrate. The Woodlawn School District, as detailed previously, went to great lengths to exclude the Black children of Lincoln Heights but still had a high percentage of Blacks (35%)
compared to that of Sharonville. If Sharonville, for example, wanted to maintain racial homogeneity, then entering a consolidation plan with Woodlawn
would upset its nearly all-White status in the present and even more so in the
future. Some anti-consolidation literature hinted at this future threat by alluding to the fact that Lincoln Heights shared borders with two of the eight districts and could easily be annexed in later years. "Annexation means that a
portion of or an entire district is annexed to an adjoining district." (Hamilton
County Board of Education, 1950, p. 4) This is indeed what happened in
1970 in what is referred to as the PSD/LHSD merger.

Excluding Lincoln Heights

During the period that the eight Princeton communities were seeking consolidation, Lincoln Heights School District was created and became a city
district; Woodlawn School District was redefined to exclude Lincoln Heights
students; and Evandale incorporated rich industrial lands that were once inhabited by Black residents, and its school district no longer included Lincoln
Heights students. The actions of the communities of Woodlawn and Evandale alone, with the sanction of the Hamilton County Board of Education,
would indicate that the Lincoln Heights district would not have been a wel-

come addition to the Princeton consolidation efforts. Though Luke (1981a) reports that Lincoln Heights asked to be excluded from the PSD consolidation, there is no indication that Lincoln Heights was ever a suggested or selected participant. In addition, though there may have been a group of Lincoln Heights citizens that communicated a request to be excluded from the consolidation, there is little reason to believe that such a group represented the wishes of the community as a whole. In fact, there is evidence that there were Lincoln Heights citizens on both sides of the issue just as in prior decades there were internal conflicts over the issue of incorporation. Moreover, there is no evidence that would suggest that even if an overwhelming majority of Lincoln Heights citizens had wanted to participate in the consolidation, the Hamilton County Board of Education and the other communities would have supported their petition or allowed their inclusion. After all, the county board was fully aware of Lincoln Heights' situation and was instrumental in bringing it about. The board had recommended the original seven districts without receiving requests or petitions. Since several of the boards of education officially objected to their districts' inclusion, it is unlikely that the Hamilton County Board of Education made their recommendations based upon a district's desire or approval. Therefore, Lincoln Heights' alleged request to be excluded after the fact does not explain their initial and final exclusion from the list of districts that would comprise the Princeton School District. While exclusion on the basis of race is rarely overtly expressed and documented in board minutes or resolutions, it may have indeed been an issue in the creation of PSD. When speaking in general of the consolidation efforts in the Cincinnati Metropolitan Area during this time period, Reed and Reed (1953) listed "...racial and social distinctions of which little is said publicly..." (p. 14), as one of the major difficulties in bringing districts together. Harris and Erickson (1952) cast aspersions on the board's role in the Woodlawn/Lincoln Heights division stating, "[t]he motives which this set of facts seem to impute to the County Board are hardly very commendable. There is also the possibility of a racial question." (p. 11) Perhaps their comment and observation would also apply the county's handling of the PSD consolidation.

PART IV

Return of the Fly to the Ointment

CHAPTER 5

Budgets and Buildings: 1955–1970

In this chapter, tax valuations, per-pupil expenditures, teacher salaries, and capital expenditures of the two school districts, PSD and LHSD are compared and contrasted.

PSD Finances

By 1955 when the Princeton Board of Education was formed, the tax valuation for the district was $65,800,000. This was an increase of $7.33 million from 1953 when the initial consolidation resolution was passed by the county board. In 1956 a $4.7 million bond issue was passed. At this time the new Princeton district was serving approximately 3,000 school-age children. (Luke, 1981b, p. 5)

After the PSD consolidation, increased enrollments in the affected local schools required some busing of students to buildings with more space. Some temporary structures were erected while plans for new construction were solidified. For example, Woodlawn, Stewart, and Runyan planned for new schools or additions to solve problems of overcrowding. As pointed out previously, only two of the eight districts offered high school grades and curricula; therefore, talk began almost immediately concerning plans to construct a new high school within the district. In 1955 architectural firms were hired, and in 1956 a local philanthropist donated land within the Springdale community as a site for the new Princeton High School, which opened in the 1958–59 academic year with approximately 950 students and 17 teachers. (Luke, 1981, p. 5) Teachers' salaries for that academic year are shown in Table 2. Table 3 shows the teacher salary schedule for the academic year just prior to the merger with Lincoln Heights.

LHSD Finances

Neighboring Lincoln Heights School District was no longer a part of the county system because the village gained city status shortly after the district

Table 2: PSD Teacher Salary Schedule Effective during 1958/59 Academic Year. Data from Luke, (1981b, p. 6).

Degree Obtained	Minimum Salary	Maximum Salary
No Degree	$3,200	$5,200
Bachelor	$4,000	$6,500
Master	$4,200	$6,700

Table 3: PSD Teacher Salary Schedule Effective during 1968/69 Academic Year. Data from Luke, (1982, p. 3).

Degree Obtained	Minimum Salary	Maximum Salary
Bachelor	$6,500	$10,010
Master	$7,150	$11,570
Doctoral	$600 above Masters	$1200 above Masters

Table 4: LHSD Teacher Salary Schedule Effective during 1968/69 Academic Year. Data from Lincoln Heights Board of Education, (1968, July 11).

Degree Obtained	Minimum Salary	Maximum Salary
No Degree	$4,800	$6,100
Bachelor	$5,800	$8,200
5th Year	$5,900	$8,492
Master	$6,100	$9,100

was created by the county board. LHSD lines coincided with its incorporated village and later its city lines and therefore included no other communities or areas in other communities. Lincoln Heights was not included in the 1953 consolidation resolution, nor was this district included in the Princeton district by 1955 as was Woodlawn. The Lincoln Heights Board of Education, in a 1970 retrospective analysis of the Lincoln Heights, Woodlawn and PDS relationship, stated:

> The history of this valley makes us akin to the Princeton School District, before its marriage for money. As late as 1950 we were a part of the Woodlawn Local School District. The division of Woodlawn and Lincoln Heights Districts is a prime example of black exploitation that must be corrected. (Lincoln Heights Seeks, 1970, p. 11)

Despite Lincoln Heights' exclusion from Woodlawn and later PDS, the financial and economic links between the newly created districts continued as late as 1957. These links were evidenced by the fact that "In December of 1957 Princeton transferred to Lincoln Heights $6,500,000 of tax valuation of the General Electric Company plant in Evandale. This doubled the tax valuation of that district and enabled them to build a new high school." (Luke, 1981b, p. 6)

There was no high school in the Lincoln Heights community; therefore, even after the Lincoln Heights School District was created in 1950, children were sent out of the district for grades 9 through 12. Many of the children attended a predominantly Black high school in the adjoining Lockland village just south of Lincoln Heights. (see Figure 5 on page 63) By 1957 the financial situation had not changed in any significant way in that the village/city had not benefited from any additional industry. Lincoln Heights could either continue to send its high school students out of the district, allowing neighboring Lockland or perhaps the new Princeton district to absorb this burden, or build a new high school. In a newspaper interview, the PSD superintendent indicated that there was talk of annexing Lincoln Heights into the PSD district but Lincoln Heights' leaders preferred to build a new high school. (City Problems, 1970) The transfer of tax valuation of the General Electric Company Plant made this possible. Lincoln Heights would then have a tax valuation of approximately $13,000,000, since the transfer reportedly doubled it. However, in a recent interview Willis Holloway, superintendent of Lincoln Heights School district at the time, adamantly refutes the claims that Lincoln Heights was invited to join the PSD district and, furthermore, refutes the notion that the tax transfer was significant enough to build a high school. (see chapter 7)

The new Lincoln Heights High School opened in September 1958 to accommodate 240 pupils. Operating this new facility in addition to the existing elementary school added stress to an already insufficient Lincoln Heights School Board budget. Comparing Lincoln Heights' financial situation to neighboring districts just a few years after the opening of the new high school gives a sense of the barriers they faced. The Lincoln Heights city/village and its school district would continue this struggle against all odds up until its merger with PSD in 1970. The limited budget of LHSD, for example, directly affected its ability to compete with PSD in attracting and retaining the most qualified and experienced teachers specifically for their new high schools. As late as the 1968/69 academic year, just prior to the merger, there was a considerable difference in salary schedules for the two districts as shown in Tables 3 and 4.

Considering the fact that the Princeton High School is less than five miles from the Lincoln Heights High School, geographic location would not likely factor in prospective teachers' choices of employment. The Princeton High School could likely attract teachers looking for a better equipped facility, a broader curriculum, professional development opportunities, and higher monetary rewards than the Lincoln Heights High School could offer. Moreover, since its creation LHSD also had to compete with other districts, such as the Cincinnati City School District, that also offered more benefits, greater resources, and higher salaries. Black teachers preferring or at least willing to work in an all-Black school system were often lost to other districts in the county or city if such opportunities presented themselves. (White teachers typically did not apply for positions in LHSD.) The situation actually worsened for LHSD through the years until just prior to the 1970 PSD/LHSD merger. In a newspaper interview concerning the ability to attract and retain teachers to support a broad curriculum, Eddie Starr, the principal of Lincoln Heights High School, stated:

> We would like to give the college preparatory student and the slow learner the special attention they need. It takes teachers certified in specialties and we can't pay them. Five years ago we could get them because no matter how good they were they had trouble getting jobs in white districts. Now it's different. The ones we had we couldn't keep. And now it's difficult to even get them. (Simms, 1970, p. 15)

Willis Holloway, Lincoln Heights' school superintendent, reiterated these same problems and concerns. "When there was no other opportunity open years ago for Negroes, we had a steady supply of teachers." (City Problems, 1970, p. 10) He also attributed the diminished number of teachers available to Lincoln Heights to the fact that Black teachers were enjoying opportunities elsewhere. Holloway points out, "it's only been in the last four years that we've employed teachers without a degree." (p. 10) Lincoln Heights High School also suffered in that one-third of its staff had college degrees but did not hold state teaching certificates. (City Problems, 1970, p. 10) Similarly, Reverend James Francis, a local Episcopalian minister and member of the Princeton Black Educational Advisory Committee, spoke concerning other limited resources that plagued Lincoln Heights' schools. "They [Lincoln

Heights] couldn't even have good schools here even if all the extra money was given to them. They don't have the facilities." (p. 15)

In the early 1950s when the Lincoln Heights School District was created as a result of a split with Woodlawn, it had a tax valuation of $1.7 million, 929 students, a per-pupil valuation of $1,929. (City Problems, 1970) These figures have more meaning when compared to Woodlawn's $2.5 million tax valuation, 178 students, and a per-pupil valuation of $14,051. The financial crisis did not improve, for by 1964 "...Lincoln Heights had $7,154 worth of property to be taxed to educate each child. It was less than half the county average and one-tenth of what St. Bernard and Lockland had available for their children." (City Problems, 1970) This Black school district had fared no better by 1969, as noted by the *Cincinnati Post & Times Star*:

> Lincoln Heights is the poorest school district in Hamilton County with a tax base of only $5,631.50 per pupil. Its operating tax rate of $21/25 per $1,000 property valuation is 17th in the list of 24 school districts and its per pupil expenditure is $435.44, third lowest of the group. (Segregation in Lincoln Heights, 1969, p. 34)

CHAPTER 6

The Merger: 1961–1970

In 1970 the Princeton School District agreed to accept approximately 1,900 Black students from the neighboring economically depressed community of Lincoln Heights, Ohio. In this chapter, the events leading up to and pertinent to the merger of PSD and LHSD are investigated.

Out and in the County

The poverty of the Lincoln Heights School District in the midst of surrounding wealth set the stage for its merger and annexation to another district. It is important to point out again that in 1961 Lincoln Heights was granted its request to give up its independent city school district status and return as a local school district under the jurisdiction of Hamilton County. (City Problems, 1970) Leaders in Lincoln Heights were fully aware of the financial crises in their schools and were active in efforts to resolve the situation. School board minutes reveal that the request to remain with/rejoin the Hamilton County School District began almost immediately after the creation of LHSD even though the request was not granted until a decade later.

> The clerk then stated that he had talked with Superintendent Crouch and Asst. Superintendent Wilson and that they suggested that our board write the county board a letter if we desired to remain under county supervision. (Lincoln Heights Board of Education Meeting Minutes, 1951, February 7)

> A communication was received from the Board of Education of the Lincoln Heights Local School District, stating that the Board wishes to remain under the supervision of the Hamilton County Board of Education. (Hamilton County Board of Education Meeting Minutes, 1951, March 13)

Once under county jurisdiction, Lincoln Heights could again benefit from county services and perhaps better position itself for annexation to neighboring county districts. Interestingly, shortly after this move by Lincoln Heights in 1961, the Princeton School District moved from county jurisdiction and became an independent city district after one of its communities, Sharonville, attained city status. Luke (1981b) reports, "This action was not mandatory, but was enacted at the discretion of the Board, giving Princeton more autonomy and saving…in contributions to the Hamilton County Board of Education." (p. 7) Despite the reasons offered by the Princeton Board and its Superintendent, Robert Lucas, some believed that Princeton's move out of county jurisdiction, almost simultaneous with Lincoln Heights' return, was not coincidental but the result of strategic planning. *The Cincinnati Enquirer* reports, "There were suspicions that the move also was made to prevent the two adjacent districts—Lincoln Heights and Princeton—from being under the county board at the same time and thus, more easily merged." (City Problems, 1970, p. 10)

Revoking the Charter

Lincoln Heights continued to struggle from 1961 through 1968 with limited resources, and no merger or annexation occurred. The factor that propelled the merger of LHSD to a neighboring district was a state action resulting in the loss of its charter and ultimate disbanding of the district. In documenting the PSD/LHSD merger, Luke (1982) begins:

> In December of 1969 the State Board of Education voted to revoke the charter of Lincoln Heights School. Martin Essex, state superintendent, listed thirty-eight standards which he said Lincoln Heights had failed to meet during three inspections made over the past two years. (p. 4)

Similarly, 1969 reports in two major Cincinnati newspapers present the loss of the charter in much the same way:

> Lincoln Heights students may be integrated into Lockland, Princeton and Wyoming next year. That was one of the alternatives which emerged here Monday after the state Board of Education revoked the Lincoln Heights local school district charter, effective June 30. The District charter was revoked because it failed to meet 38 minimum state standards. There was no opposition to the charter revocation Monday. (Wheat, 1969, p. 20)

> Officials of Lincoln Heights, Lockland, Princeton and Wyoming school districts and the State Board of Education will meet Friday, Dec. 19 to discuss where Lincoln

Heights students will attend school next year. The state board voted unanimously to revoke the charter of the Lincoln Heights Local School District yesterday because it failed to meet 38 state minimum standards. (Robinson, 1969, p. 12)

The Lincoln Heights Response

The reader of these accounts might falsely assume that the Lincoln Heights community and school board were passive participants, recipients, or victims of this state action. However, a newspaper serving the Mill Creek Valley communities painted a different picture of involvement in its reports both before and after the charter revocation. According to the *Mill Creek Valley News:*

> Three weeks ago...[we] revealed that this may be the last year of operation of the district, since the *Lincoln Heights Board of Education had passed a resolution asking that the district be dissolved.*...[L]ast week the United States Department of Justice had issued an order calling for the dissolving of Lincoln Heights School District. However,...the Ohio Department of Education requested and gained approval to instigate a thorough study of the situation prior to any formal action. (emphasis added; State and Local Leaders, 1969, p. 2)

> Several months ago, the *Lincoln Heights Board of Education asked that the school district be dissolved* to pave the way for merger with neighboring districts. Monday, that request was granted when the Ohio Board of Education revoked the district's charter to operate in Ohio, effective June 30, 1970. (emphasis added; County, Lockland, 1969, p. 1)

School board minutes as well as later reports in the major newspapers (e.g., Small Tax Base, 1970) verify that Lincoln Heights' citizens and leaders were not only involved in the events that so affected their futures but actually initiated them. The state gained its power to revoke the Lincoln Heights charter from legislation, Senate Bill 350, passed in 1967, that allowed the state to dissolve and merge districts. (City Problems, 1970) The Lincoln Heights School Board was aware of this bill and the power it gave to the state. School board minutes document communication initiated by the Lincoln Heights Board of Education with the Hamilton County Board of Education asking for a state evaluation of the Lincoln Heights schools. A letter from the LHSD superintendent states that an evaluation of Lincoln Heights' schools would reveal that the district lacks resources to meet the state standards and the ability to provide a quality education to the students. The letter goes on to suggest that LHSD be joined with one of the neighboring districts under the power of the new legislation, SB 350. (Lincoln Heights Board of Education Meeting Minutes, 1968, February 8)

The Lincoln Heights Board continued to initiate communication with both state and county officials after the evaluation request. The state's April 1969 evaluation concluded that the educational programs provided in Lincoln Heights' schools were vastly inadequate, particularly its high school programs, and suggested the consolidation of LHSD with other districts. After receiving a copy of the evaluation report in July 1969, the Lincoln Heights Board drafted a letter to the county superintendent and a resolution that reflected their support of the state's conclusions. (Lincoln Heights Board of Education Meeting Minutes, 1969, July 12)

Threat of Suit

The July resolution drafted by the Lincoln Heights Board also indicated that other Lincoln Heights citizens, non-board members, were very concerned about the plight of their community and its institutions and suggested feelings of impatience and discontent. Addressing this issue directly during the July 12, 1969, Lincoln Heights Board of Education Meeting, Superintendent Willis Holloway wrote:

> Without reflecting threat or intimidation of any kind, I must point out the growing unrest, internally and externally regarding the historical inequities involving Lincoln Heights School District. (Lincoln Heights Board of Education Meeting Minutes, 1969, July 12)

Indeed this was no idle threat, for Lincoln Heights citizens were later credited in *The Cincinnati Enquirer* with propelling the consolidation talks initiated by the Lincoln Heights Board:

> A group of Lincoln Heights citizens provided the spark. They filed a complaint with the Justice Department's Civil Rights Division saying that Lincoln Heights students were not getting the best education because of gerrymandering of tax boundary lines and resultant de facto segregation. The complaint brought about a threatened law suit under the Civil Rights Act of 1964 from the Justice Department. (Community Gives, 1970, p. 7A)

> In February 1969, justice officials talked to the State Education Department about resolving the problem. The state school board, faced for the first time with a choice

of acting or getting sued, ordered state administrators to get moving. (Small Tax
Base, 1970, p. 25)

The impact that citizen activism had on the course of events is reflected
in the fact that Hamilton county and Ohio state officials met in August 1969
to discuss problems of poverty and segregation in Lincoln Heights schools
and possible remedies. (Segregation in Lincoln Heights, 1969) An early
newspaper article reported State Superintendent Martin Essex saying "...the
Justice Dept. in Washington has been interested in the Lincoln Heights District and its problems for more than a year because of the fact that the district
includes practically 100 percent Negro students." (County, Lockland, 1969,
p. 1) Similarly, assistant State Superintendent Thomas Quick alluded to a suit
under the Civil Rights act in stating that "[n]ot the least of the problems...is
that in addition to being a district stricken by poverty Lincoln Heights is almost 100 per cent Negro, making it also an integration problem." (Robinson,
1969, p. 12) Though Superintendent Essex later denied the importance of the
Justice Department's interest or the threat of a lawsuit, State Superintendent
Robert Greer admitted that a federal lawsuit was "...a definite possibility
because of inequities and inadequacies cited by the federal investigation and
confirmed by the state evaluation. He noted that federal officials preferred a
voluntary solution." (Small Tax Base, 1970, p. 25) Robert Lucas, superintendent of Princeton Schools, provided further insight into the lawsuit threat
beyond the fact that Lincoln Heights was a poor all-Black village and school
district. According to Lucas, "The Justice Department believed it had a case
against Princeton because Lincoln Heights was once part of the Woodlawn
district, which later joined to help form Princeton and that the separation of
Lincoln Heights from Woodlawn had been improper." (as cited in Robinson,
1970b, p. 7) In any case, it is difficult to deny the fact that the "merger talks
initiated by Holloway in 1968 picked up tempo after the Federal suit threat."
(Small Tax Base, 1970, P. 25)

A Citizens Committee

A Lincoln Heights' citizens committee, The Project Committee, was also
instrumental in involving fellow residents through surveys and increasing
community interest in improving the educational system in Lincoln Heights.
(Small Tax Base, 1970, p. 25) The three surveys administered by The Project
Committee revealed that a major reason prominent citizens had left Lincoln

Heights was its inadequate schools, that a small percentage of graduates of Lincoln Heights High School since 1959 had successful careers, and that 90% of the survey sample favored consolidation. (Small Tax Base, 1970, p. 25) The Project Committee also initiated communication and dialogue with local, state, and federal officials prior to the 1969 charter revocation.

The Final Decision

The decision to revoke the Lincoln Heights' charter came down December 8, 1969, from the Ohio State Board of Education and, as noted above, most initial reports did not reveal the involvement of citizens in the Lincoln Heights community. *The Cincinnati Enquirer* reported: "Dr. Martin Essex, superintendent of public instruction, said the charter was revoked 'because we are concerned at the lack of quality education available to the children of Lincoln Heights School District.'" (Wheat, 1969, p. 20) The Lincoln Heights Local School Board of Education, in fact, supported the findings of the evaluation report that purported the failure of its schools to meet minimum standards and revealed this support in a special meeting held December 2, 1969, six days prior to the state's official decision. In this special meeting, the Lincoln Heights Board adopted a resolution to be forwarded to state officials notifying them that no hearing on the matter will be requested, and, furthermore, the Lincoln Heights Board would not dispute the state's decision should they revoke the Lincoln Heights charter. (Lincoln Heights Board of Education (Special) Meeting Minutes, 1969, December 2) Since the revocation of the charter would essentially mean the disbandment of LHSD, the next step would be to decide which district or districts would absorb the school-age children. Again the Lincoln Heights board encouraged all with power and responsibility to propel consolidation efforts forward. At this same meeting, the members voted to "go on record as using extreme discretion regarding any communication on the State Evaluation Report." (Lincoln Heights Board of Education (Special) Meeting Minutes, 1969, December 2) It seems the Lincoln Heights Board was deliberately maintaining a low profile and keeping their involvement in potential school consolidation out of the public eye. (Lincoln Heights Board of Education (Special) Meeting Minutes, 1969, December 2)

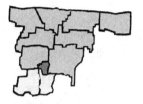

The Next Step

A 1970 *Mill Creek Valley News* article reported the following:

> After revoking the Lincoln Heights School charter, the State Board of Education
> was presented with four different plans that would assure boys and girls of the city a
> quality education. The various plans concern Lincoln Heights, Princeton, Lockland
> and Wyoming. (No "Demands," 1970)

Various reports indicated that Lincoln Heights school-age children may be assigned to two or more neighboring districts; additional resources may be supplied or industrial properties transferred to Lincoln Heights to bring the schools up to standards and allow the renewal of its charter, or Lincoln Heights may merge or annex to a neighboring district. (Robinson, 1969; Wheat, 1969) Meetings were held with state and county officials and administrators in the four districts involved in order to discuss options for educating the Lincoln Heights children after the disbandment of LHSD. Lincoln Heights' leaders requested that all the children in their community be assigned to the same district, ruling out one or more of the possible options presented to the board. The provision of additional resources or the transfer of industrial property to reinstate the Lincoln Heights charter would likely not satisfy the Justice Department and its concerns over a segregated Black district. *The Cincinnati Enquirer* speculated: "Had the talks not begun, the Cincinnati community may have been the subject of a federal suit demanding integration of schools much like what has taken place in other in parts of the United States." (Community Gives, 1970, p. 7A)

The most likely option to be adopted by the County Board was the merger or annexation of Lincoln Heights to another district. Annexation required that the portions of the districts' boundaries coincide. At this time Lincoln Heights District boundaries coincided with those of Princeton to the north and northeast, Lockland to the south, and Wyoming at the southwestern tip, hence the reason for involving the four districts in the talks.

Though local leaders and county officials met several times to devise an agreed-upon solution to the Lincoln Heights problem, the state maintained absolute veto power. The state gained its authority from Ohio law, 3301-16 of the Ohio Revised Code, which gave it discretionary power and control when a district is dissolved. (Robinson, 1970b) The desire was to reach a permanent solution that all districts involved could accept, yet the solution had to satisfy the federal Justice Department from which the state was receiving pressure. Robert Lucas, Princeton superintendent, stated, "During all this time U.S. Justice Department lawyers were in our office and in close contact with the state Department of Education, and they said to me that if the state did not settle it, they would." (as cited in Robinson, 1970b, p. 7)

After the Merger

The consensus of opinion among the leaders in the Princeton and Lincoln Heights consolidation was that the merger was successful. Despite the racist attitudes and policies that created these segregated communities and districts, desegregation was accomplished with relative peace and ease. The Princeton School District went from a 12% Black enrollment to a 20%–30% Black student body from 1970 to 1975. Eddie L. Starr, principal of Lincoln Heights High School prior to the merger, associate principal of the consolidated Princeton High School, and associate superintendent of the consolidated district, reflected on the success of this desegregation effort and said "The people around here are proud of our programs and our awards....They love the football team and the chorus and the marching band. But they don't seem to talk much about what a great thing we've all done in pulling off the merger." (cited in Wheeler, 1996, p. 19) Robert Lucas, the superintendent of the Princeton School District before, during, and after the merger, attributes much of its success to the commitment of the Princeton Board of Education:

> The Princeton Board of Education passed a resolution which stated in part that "we accept the challenge of this responsibility, and we urge that the Lincoln Heights School District be brought into full membership in the Princeton School District and the Princeton superintendent and his staff be directed to use all of their many talents to provide the children of the enlarged school district the same high academic opportunities that the Princeton children have enjoyed since the inception of the district." (Lucas, 1976, p. 3)

The prime key to success is a board of education that is solidly committed to the principle of desegregating and eventually integrating the school system and that will stay together to provide the leadership and financial resources to do the job. (p. 9)

During an interview I conducted, Starr, who had later retired as associate superintendent of PSD, agreed with Lucas's assessment of the reasons for the smooth transfer and transition of students. According to Starr, "…Princeton fought tooth and nail to keep us from being merged, however, to their credit, to the Board of Education and to Dr. Lucas' credit, once it was determined that the merger was going to take place, they did everything they could to make it work." (personal communication, March 13, 2001)

While nonviolent, peaceful racial integration of the schools was the desired goal, educational outcomes were also seen as important measures of the success of this desegregation effort. One of the great fears held by those already in the Princeton district was that academic standards would suffer throughout the system after the admittance of the Lincoln Heights students. Consequently, the Princeton school administration took many steps to combat this fear and to assure that it would not become a reality. A variety of courses and programs were added to the curriculum; teaching and support staffs were increased and racially integrated; and significant in-service programs were offered. (Lucas, 1976) Table 5 shows the results of standardized tests given to elementary students the year of the merger, before the arrival of the Black Lincoln Heights students, and the scores for five subsequent years. The performances of groups of students are compared to the national norms for their respective grade levels with the plus (+) or minus (-) signs indicating the number of months the students performed above or below the national norm. Lucas claims, "Generally speaking, the academic achievement of the Princeton students was higher five years after the merger than it was before the merger." (p. 7) The outcomes data available for those years do not reveal the effect that desegregation had on the performance of the African American students alone. What the data do reveal is the effects of desegregation on the student body as a whole. Of course, it is doubtful that the mere presence of Black students brought about these changes. However, the fears attached to desegregation and the anxiety caused by the presence of significantly more Black students in an historically White school district caused administrators to pour more educational resources into the district and provide greater educational opportunities for all students. The plan worked.

When increased opportunities and challenges are offered students, regardless of race or ethnicity, their performance and achievement will also rise. (see Darling-Hammond, 2000)

Table 5: Princeton District Stanford Achievement Test Results for the Elementary Grades. Data from Lucas, R. E., (1976).

PSD Stanford Achievement Test Results						
Year	Months Above (+) or Below (-) National Average					
	3rd Grade	4th Grade	5th Grade	6th Grade	7th Grade	8th Grade
69–70	+5	+5	+6	+6	+7	+6
70–71	+1	+2	-2	0	0	-1
71–72	+3	0	0	-3	-1	-5
72–73	+3	+3	+4	+5	+4	+4
73–74	+9	+6	+8	+6	+7	+3
74–75	+9	+8	+9	+8	+2	+4

Another educational outcome that is often used as a measure of success for secondary schools is the level of postsecondary education sought by graduates. In the case of Princeton High School, this measure also went up after the merger. Wheeler (1996) reports, "Whereas just over 40 percent of Princeton graduates had gone on to advanced educational programs in 1970, in 1975 that figure had escalated to 60 percent." (p. 19) One would assume that this increase was also due to the enrichment programs and the numerous course offerings that were added to the Princeton curriculum as a result of the merger. Six years after the merger, Lucas (1976) states, "The high school program showed the same pattern as the elementary. Course offerings were expanded in all areas, and Princeton now offers more than 265 courses." (p. 7)

It is interesting to note that the data on the performance of the Black Lincoln Heights students after desegregation were either not gathered or not published. Desegregation was deemed a success based solely on the outcome of the total student body, the majority of whom were, of course, White. The implication was that, when measuring success, the focus was not on whether African American achievement went up but on whether their presence negatively affected the performance of the White majority. There is a measure of interest convergence in this thinking. Desegregation was forced upon the Princeton District because of the vast inequities in the Lincoln Heights District. Those who worked to bring about the merger saw justice finally coming to the children of Lincoln Heights. But justice only came after significant steps were in place to assure that the White majority would benefit. Success of desegregation was measured not by the eradication of previous injustices and inequities but by its effect upon the White majority.

PART V

"Back in the Day"
Looking Inside the Schools and Lives of Educators during the Segregation and Desegregation of the Lincoln Heights (Ohio) School District

CHAPTER 7

The Administrators

Four hours of interview data are converted into a biographical sketch of Willis Holloway, who served as a teacher and high school principal at Lincoln Heights High School prior to accepting the position of superintendent of the Lincoln Heights School District. His involvement in the merger of the two districts, PSD and LHSD, was of key importance. In this interview Holloway provides insight into the political climate during the time of the merger.

Eddie Lawrence Starr provided three hours of interview data, also sharing insights into the social, economic, and political climate that prevailed in the upper Mill Creek (Ohio) valley in the 1960s prior to the PSD/LHSD merger. Starr served as a high school teacher before becoming principal of Lincoln Heights High School. After the merger, he continued work in the new Princeton School District and later became the first African American associate superintendent in the district, where he remained until retirement. Starr was student centered throughout his career as educator and was able to share concerns and perspectives of the students under his tutelage and counsel.

An hour of interview data provides adequate information to develop a biographical sketch of Ernest Ector. Beginning as a biology teacher, Ector eventually became principal of the Lincoln Heights Elementary School. He remained in this position after the merger of the two districts until his retirement.

Willis Holloway
Superintendent Lincoln Heights Public Schools, 1961–1969
Associate Superintendent Cincinnati Public Schools, 1970–1988

Educational Background

I was born in Cincinnati according to my birth certificate, but my family moved to the Lincoln Heights area very early on.[1] My grandfather was one of the early settlers of Lincoln Heights—mud streets and all—so I grew up out here, obviously. I went to what was then called South Woodlawn School, which is significant in this discussion. South Woodlawn Elementary was segregated—very much so. From there, I attended Lockland Wayne, where most of the graduates from Lincoln Heights Elementary (South Woodlawn Elementary) went. That was in an era when the state paid tuition for school districts that had no high schools. The young people could go to any one of the neighboring high schools, and the state paid the tuition. There were a few kids who went to Glendale; Wyoming didn't take too many, but maybe one or two got into Wyoming; some went to Hughes I can remember that. But anyway, the state paid the tuition—and of course that changed. From there I graduated from high school.

I attended St. Xavier in New Orleans. I transferred in my sophomore year to Philander Smith College, which is a Methodist school in Little Rock, Arkansas, because I had several "homies" from this community going to school there. They talked me into transferring over there; this was one of the few times in my life when I did something because of somebody else. They were football players and were at Philander on football scholarships. I was at New Orleans at the time. They came down to play Dillard, which was in New Orleans, and I went over to see the game. The basketball coach happened to have been with them on the trip. They told him a little bit about Lockland Wayne and my history, so he offered me a basketball scholarship to transfer. I had played basketball at Lockland Wayne High School. It was a small school so you played whatever they had. Basketball was the big sport, of course, but I played football and a little baseball. So I transferred and graduated from Philander Smith College in 1954.

I then went to the University of Arkansas on a Ford scholarship. That is significant because it was a special kind of a scholarship wherein they were conducting a study to determine how to develop the best teachers. Traditionally, people who went to school for majors in education had a major in a subject area and a minor in education—professional courses. However, this study was designed to take people who did not have that background—who graduated from an undergraduate school without that background—and give them the professional courses as graduate students. I had a double major when I graduated, psychology, of all things, and physical education. I received my masters degree in education through that process, and from there I entered teaching here at Lincoln Heights. Ultimately in 1975 I got my doctorate in education administration. That is the educational background and the path that I have woven. I have been to many schools including the University of Cincinnati and Miami University.

From Teacher to Principal to Superintendent

I returned to Lincoln Heights in the fall of 1954, which was the year that I spent at the University of Arkansas. Late in the year, perhaps as late as September, I got a call from a very close personal friend. He asked if I would leave school and come to take a job in Lincoln Heights. Actually, he had accepted this same job in Lincoln Heights but had subsequently gotten another offer from Cincinnati[2] that paid much more money. He wanted to take the Cincinnati job, but Lincoln Heights wouldn't release him from the contract unless he got someone to replace him. I agreed to come home and do that, which freed him to take the job in Cincinnati. That is how I ended up back here.

I was teaching junior high school. At the time Lincoln Heights Elementary School went up through eighth grade, and I was teaching seventh and eighth graders for the most part. I was teaching a special class in health and physical education. The kids rotated through my classroom like they did for most special classes—music, art, physical education. I taught those classes until 1960, when I was named principal of the high school. And shortly thereafter, actually the next year, I was named superintendent of the district.

How I became superintendent is a strange but interesting story. The board had fired the superintendent, for whatever reason. I do not know what the reasons were. He was a Harvard graduate, of all things, and I don't know how he got way back down to Lincoln Heights. Anyway, they fired him, but they did not have anybody particular in mind to serve as a replacement. Now you have to keep in mind that during that era there were a lot of county schools; there are no county schools anymore. Lincoln Heights Schools had just recently gone into the county system, which technically meant we were under the county superintendent. There is no such animal anymore; there is no county superintendent in this county. (They called those local districts.) They did not have anyone in mind to replace the fired superintendent; it turned out that I had some advocates on the board, and I was the only one with the superintendent certificate. And to my shock, I casually walked into the building one day—I have forgotten what I was going down there for—and a fellow met me coming out of the door. He said, "Congratulations." I said, "What are you talking about?" He said, "You're the superintendent." I said, "Oh, you're kidding. What are you talking about?" They had appointed me superintendent and that is how I became the superintendent. That was in 1961. I stayed there until I went to Cincinnati Public Schools in 1970.

Lincoln Heights School District: Separating from Woodlawn

Let me give you this history in reverse. The people who were planning to create Princeton, including Bob Lucas, could foresee things because they were doing the planning, that obviously folk from Cincinnati did not appreciate and could not see. So some folks sold the Lincoln Heights group and its leader, Luther Lyle, a "bill of goods." He was a "big" man here in Lincoln Heights at the time, and he felt like it. As a matter of fact—this is kind of funny—he used to tell me all the time that he was the richest man in Lincoln Heights. He said that if you have $12,000 in the bank and you do not owe anybody anything, you are rich. I think about that now; it is so funny. He owned four corners of an intersection, which is one reason he thought he was rich. He had a store on one corner, and he lived on another. The two-story house is still there; different people lived there over the years.[3]

Anyway, he was the guy, if I had to say somebody sold the thing down the river. I gave him a bad time about his lack of foresight, but as an adult I came to realize that he was aging at the time and I should not have mistreated him. I do not know who the people were that called him in, but they called him in for a meeting. He had a couple of other people with him and convinced them that it was going to be in their vested interest to run their own school district. At that time we were under the Woodlawn Board of Education, that is why we were named South Woodlawn. The school that used to be located on Wayne Avenue, very close to the corner of Marion and Wayne, was called North Woodlawn. (North Woodlawn School has since been torn down.) We were under the Woodlawn district, which was under the county. Those people knew what was going to happen, so they convinced Lyle and others by saying, "You ought to run your own school district." Woodlawn did not pull out; they talked Lincoln Heights into pulling out.[4]

One of the best resources you can have politically on this issue would be Guy Westmoreland. He was the youngest of the politicians who were up front in all of the political activities. They were trying to incorporate and were the ones who fought the battle, which is a different story but related. They could get no justice in the courts; records could not be found; General Electric was taken and given to Evandale, and on, and on, and on.[5] They were fighting that battle while, at the same time, certain people convinced Lyle that he needed to run his own school system. This community was then convinced that controlling its school system was the way it should go. Because the community had to vote on the issue, Lincoln Heights actually isolated itself in that regard.

The Original Princeton School District Consolidation: Lincoln Heights Exclusion

But at the time of the Lincoln Heights and Woodlawn separation there had been no mention of Princeton merging. That was not an option. That was not an issue. It was not even a discussion at that time.[6] Just a few short years later, I do not remember the exact dates, the merger[7] did surface and then, "ah-h." Then it came to light why it happened the way it happened. You may or may not have experienced some of the racism, both perceived and real, that occurred between communities.[8] Take a community like Sharonville. There are Blacks that live there now, but Sharonville was one of those communities in which Blacks were just hated, you might say. The Reading community was another one. In fact, it was true of all the contiguous communities, but Sharonville more than most. Nevertheless, Sharonville was one of the leading districts pushing for the merger, and Sharonville had a lot of racists up there. So Lucas was not going to be able to pull a merger off that included Lincoln Heights without a political or legal fight of some kind. In any case, they maneuvered and got Lincoln Heights out of the picture.

Now a couple of other things happened that helped that process. One was Lincoln Heights, somehow, came up with a census that said we had 5,000 people. (I do not think we have ever had 5,000 people in Lincoln Heights.) Because they came up with a census that said we had 5,000 people meant we would become a city. And it was a city without resources and without the capacity to grow and the ability to serve its people. But again, it is amazing when you are hurting yourself what people will let you do. All these laws were there but we were just hurting ourselves. No one questioned it, so Lincoln Heights became a city. And Lincoln Heights was further isolated because the educational laws that govern cities are very different. However, the county was happy. The county superintendent was extremely happy because it took him off the hook. He was going to be on the hook because he was going to have to account for the fact that he had this little isolated, island-like district out there and he did not seem to be doing anything about it. But once

Lincoln Heights became a city, a new set of laws freed him up. Now they backed that up with the coup de grâce. They got Sharonville to immediately vote to become a city. They have always had the people but, like Glendale, they did not want it. Glendale does not want to be a city; it wants to be a unique, quaint residential village. And this is what it is. But Glendale is growing. It has some beautiful new homes there now, but they never mention statistics. They do not want to become a city. Sharonville was the same way. Now, of course, it is a big city with all the industry that is there. But the industry was not there at the time though the potential was there. But nevertheless, they immediately declared, "We are a city." So the district became the Princeton City School District versus the Princeton Local School District. Had it been a local school district, then the county superintendent, in those days, could have recommended to the state superintendent that the configuration of the merger would be different. It would have been that simple.[9] I could be wrong about the timeline but I do not think so. The people orchestrating the merger were aware of the laws and knew early on that as long as they were accountable to the county superintendent, they were vulnerable. The answer to overcoming that vulnerability was making any one of those communities a city. Sharonville was the most likely candidate; it had the most people so it was willing to take it on. The moment that occurred, no matter what Lincoln Heights did, the county could not do anything about it. In other words, the county could not summarily, by state law, take Lincoln Heights and put it into Princeton school district for whatever reasons, because Princeton was a city school district. The law also required that for city school districts to merge with other school districts, there had to be a referendum. I believe that law still exists. Consequently, that's how they protected themselves, and that is why it is Princeton City School District.[10]

As far as the rationale offered by Princeton administrators for changing to city status, oh yes, they gave beautiful spins on it all. Obviously this is easy to do that when you are dealing with a community like Lincoln Heights with little or no clout—no political clout.[11] Plus there is a mentality that exists, a racial mentality, that assumes that what is happening in an all-Black situation is below standard anyway and that somebody is helping them. It is a condescending kind of activity that says, "Gee, they're going to help these people in some kind way." All of that was prevalent and operative at the time.

Lincoln Heights was purposely excluded. I guess the most direct phrase would have been, "they were purposely excluded."[12] Luther Lyle, and maybe one or two other persons at the most in the Lincoln Heights community, would have wanted to be excluded from the Princeton merger. Luther Lyle was on the Woodlawn School Board then. There were always one or two Black representatives on the board, but it was mostly White. That is when Lyle was sold a bill of goods, and then he got one or two other people to sell a bill of goods. And let's face it, in a community like Lincoln Heights, there were not many politically active people or politically conscious and savvy people. It is somewhat better now but not a great deal better. However, at the time, people in the community would just go along with a man like Lyle who was thought to be the man in charge. Most of the people were struggling and trying to survive and were not very conscious of those kinds of issues. But the most important ingredient that we cannot forget is, they did not have the option of merge or run your own school system. That was never an option. That is what is critical. But concerning Lincoln Heights running its own school system, Lyle, who was on the Woodlawn Board of Education as Lincoln Heights' representative, sold this bill of goods to the few people who were politically active in the community, and they, in turn, sold it to the community. And it was just a sell. It was a sell put on to say, "Gee, this makes you powerful. You run your own thing." That took place before the merger became public.

I am being redundant, but I must keep stressing the fact that even with the limitations that the community operated under, they did not have the knowledge and the option to vote on controlling their own district versus a new big merger that was about to take place. They knew nothing about the original Princeton consolidation/merger, but it was in the making.[13]

Incorporation Boundaries and Battles

The incorporation of Lincoln Heights occurred at the time that the fight was going on about boundaries, when Evandale got General Electric. Well, we had been previously cut out of the GE property only to the extent that the word among politicians was that Lincoln Heights was attempting to incorporate.[14] The talk that was going on was, "The only way you are going to save that valuable property—that one piece of property that could have been to Lincoln Heights like Proctor and Gamble was initially to St. Bernard—is to quickly activate people in Evandale." Their incorporation was just slightly ahead of Lincoln Heights. In any case, as far as time goes, it is not like they had been incorporated for forty years. The decisions about land and the legal cases about land occurred simultaneously with Lincoln Heights attempting to merge, because one of the first things you think about when you talk about obtaining a merger, incorporating, is your boundaries.[15]

A picture of Lincoln Heights' surrounding boundaries, taken from above, looks like a jagged seashell you would pick up at the beach. It doesn't look like anything else in this country, I believe, when you start talking about boundaries. Most often, boundaries are determined by something natural, but there are no natural boundaries in Lincoln Heights on any side. Whenever it benefited others, it was cut in here; it was cut in there.[16] Talk about justice or, rather, injustice. The incorporation of Lockland is a good example of how Lincoln Heights' boundaries were cut. Lockland was not a very large place and did not have many people, but it was allowed to incorporate and come all the way up the hill on Wayne Avenue; all the way up to where Guy lives.[17] That is about as ridiculous as anything you can think of. It just does not make any kind of logical sense, if you want to apply logic. It doesn't make any sense to have a legal boundary like that.

The Building of Lincoln Heights High School

The timing for the opening of the high school was designed perfectly. And here again, T. J. Malone sold the community a bill of goods that it could support a high school. He was the superintendent and an infamous name to come through this community—a Texan that blew through here. I said "in-famous" because he was a character if there ever was one.

The state was not going to pay the tuition for students to attend schools outside their district any longer. At the same time, there was a law saying you had to go to school within the boundaries of your school district. I do not know whether it was the same law or whether there were two separate laws.[18] Lincoln Heights would have had to pay for those students to go to whatever school they were admitted to. However, once the law solidified the fact that you had to go to school in the political boundaries of your school district, Lockland, for example no longer could take students. No one could take students. Even if Lincoln Heights were paying, by state law other districts were not to take their students. Students were supposed to go to school in the district in which they lived.

There were a few more districts around the state, by the way, in similar situations. As a matter of fact, there were somewhat interesting parallels in a district called Spencer that had a similar experience with Toledo, Ohio. This was significant because the Spencer situation had a tremendous influence on the attitude of the state superintendent. Martin Essex had just gone through that messy, messy, messy fight. Ours was not messy, but that one was messy. And he wasn't about to go through two messy fights in his administration. I won't talk about that now, but I will discuss it later.

Anyway, I am saying those two laws together forced all the little districts to merge, and in situations where they were palatable, a lot of mergers took place. White folk merging with White folk. Economic groupings of people coming together. No problem. But there was never going to be a merger—I am just being facetious to make a point—that would bring Lockland and Lincoln Heights together. To put it another way, not even Lockland and Wyoming would merge because Wyoming did not want any part of Lockland. But that would have taken referendums.

The Princeton districts were just ahead of the law, but they were also in position—with the help of politicians, because politicians generally come from upper-middle-class kinds of communities—to know that opportunities for development were just tremendous. In other words, it was going to be a wealthy school district. It was not just beating the law.[19] It was not just like scraping up something and throwing something together as Malone did here to say that we, Lincoln Heights, were meeting the expectations of the law. They had the opportunity to build a tremendous school district, which I have to give Bob Lucas credit for. He put together a heck of a school district. Lincoln Heights would have contributed about 1,500 kids to the whole Princeton district, which was not very large at the time. This was a significant statistic. Woodlawn brought enough Blacks, but to add us…. So they said, "Oh no, we have got to cut this cancer out before we get this piece together."

Malone came from Texas and was hired as superintendent at Lincoln Heights. He stressed the fact that the law required that the community have its own high school, and, secondly, he convinced the community that it could afford it. "By 1956 our kids are not going to have any place to go to school." That is the kind of thing you might say if you are trying to play to people's emotions. I cannot give you the exact timing of the transfer of money from Princeton, but it could not begin to build a high school.[20] Money sounds big when you're talking about a duplicate. But what you get from a duplicate is what it yields in terms of actual tax dollars, which is much, much less. To build a high school, even as small as that one was, you have to have a tax bond levy passed, which is what happened. T. J. Malone sold the community on a bond levy, and that is what built the high school. I thought about it after getting your list of questions, and I have to admit that I cannot remember the minute circumstances surrounding that transfer. It could be thought of as magnanimous; you have got to give them that. But it was a drop in the bucket that had no bearing on anything of significance that happened to the Lincoln Heights district. It was not like someone sat at a board table at Princeton and said, "Hey, let's give Lincoln Heights 'x' number of dollars." I am not sure exactly how it happened, surely it was a little bit more than that, but its coming had no direct bearing on any of the significant things that have occurred in this community. Anyone with common sense would know that if you reduce it from its original form to dollars and cents coming in, it would not have paid for very much. It sounded much better than it ultimately wound up.

Industries, particularly industries of magnitude like General Electric and Proctor and Gamble, tell the government what they are going to pay. Not like us poor people who are audited by the government. The way the law is written, they tell the government where they have valuables and where they do not have valuables. Their accountants do all of that. Guy could tell you; he was one of the accountants at one time, you know. I don't know whether he worked on taxes, but I'm saying that's what they're allowed to do.

The statement that Lincoln Heights did not want to merge is an out-and-out lie. I am not saying that they wanted to merge; I am saying that they never had the opportunity to make a decision about merging. That was part of the spin, and I have to give Lucas credit. Maybe if I were looking at it from his point of view and trying to keep his power block solidified and everybody happy.... Because, as you can imagine, any group of people that you bring together is a problem by itself. When you get something in the mix that is a bit unusual, that makes it even worse. To really generalize, Glendale and Sharonville kinds of folks did not mix. "Who is going to run this thing? Who is going to be on this board?" That has flattened out a little bit now, but they saw the overabundance of Black folks suddenly coming into the district as the most threatening thing of all. Black folk in this community never had the choice until this last merger came along. They had some choice when the 1970 merger actually occurred. I implemented that process so I know they had some choice. But that was not really a legal choice either; it was more of an emotional choice. I will explain that later, but the choice had to do with the actual merger that took place.

I am not sure who the group of people were that got together to start thinking seriously about creating this new Princeton district because I was not party to it.[21] My guess is that Lucas was brought in as a consultant because no other name ever surfaced around leading that district but his. It was like he put the district together himself. Now granted, the decisions had to be made by politicians because you had communities coming together, political entities coming together. But he was their educational consultant, and nobody else was ever considered for the superintendency. There was no advertisement such as "Oh, we have a new district coming up here and we want to hire a superintendent, so folks from Texas and New York and everywhere else can apply." There was not anything like that.

So Lucas became God. I hate to use that expression, but he really did, and he was very much thought of that way. My dealings with Lucas started when we, Lincoln Heights, started the last initiative to bring a merger.[22] I knew who he was but I did not have any significant contact. I would see him in meetings because he was a superintendent and I was a superintendent for a short period of time, but we had no direct business prior to 1968.

Initiating the Merger

I was principal for a year and then was named superintendent, but I was both superintendent and principal for a year. People advised me not to accept the superintendency. "This thing will kill you," they said, and gave me all the reasons why I should not take it. Well, I guess it was a dream, a small dream. I just felt that I knew the community well enough and had enough training that I could deal with the internal body politics without being killed by it. I won't get into personalities, but the way the Lincoln Heights School Board functioned, particularly, was a dogfight itself. I just felt that I could deal with it. It is like they say you get a call from God, so I decided to take it in spite of the way I came into it. I did not apply for it, but it was given to me and I decided to take it.

That is when I went out and I started looking for people to make a difference. I guess it was a dream, a small dream. I immediately went out and did something that, professionally, they recommend you do not do most of the time. That is, in looking for what I thought were people that could team with me to do what had to be done, I turned to my very close friends—a person like Mr. Ector, who lives next door; we grew up together but he was not in education. He was a science major who worked in the health department. And Mr. Starr worked for the domestic relations judge. I went down and said, "Hey, I need a good man." But he did have a social studies background, and I initially brought him in as a social studies teacher. And you could get temporary certificates and then work to make them permanent. "I need a good man; you are a good person to do the kind of things we have to do considering what we are faced with." I convinced him. And he, of course, being local had some of the same feelings that I had. We both had strong feelings about the situation, and here was an opportunity to do something about it. I talked him into leaving his job, and I named him high school principal. I could then give up one of the two jobs I was holding.

Obviously, like a neophyte tends to do, I jumped in with all four feet, so to speak, trying to create things and make things happen, and I felt good about some of the kinds of things we were able to do as an extremely poor school district. But there were a couple of dynamics that were insurmountable.[23] One of them was maintaining a core staff, because as Cincinnati became more and more integrated and its policy changed and they were hiring more and more Black teachers, basically all we were doing was filtering teachers through us to Cincinnati. I used to tease Wendall Pierce, who was the superintendent down there. I call him the last of the gods because he was the last superintendent in the city who just sat in his office and could call the shots. After that superintendents caught hell in all cities, Cincinnati not being any different. But I used to say to him, "You've got to send me a stipend for training your teachers." We would get a lot of applications, particularly from southern states, because at that time school districts weren't hiring Black teachers and were not integrating. Therefore, we got a lot of applicants from Black colleges, and we had a pretty good choice of applicants. But they would move right on to Cincinnati because they would get 'x' number of thousand dollars more. So they would teach there for a year or so and move on.

There was no way to stop that bleeding without some source, an economic source that was stable. And like I said, this community has no place to grow, and there is a limit to how much taxes you can ask. Now Wyoming didn't want any industry because it is an upper-middle-class community. So it pays extremely high school taxes. Whenever they wanted to improve their schools, they had to go to the taxpayers and say, "We need you to add another fifty dollars to your tax bill," which they would gladly do. Because they were getting the kind of homogeneous school that they wanted, they would pay for it. When you move to Wyoming you know that, you know that kind of thing, but you cannot do that in Lincoln Heights. First of all, the property itself, for the most part, is not worth that much. It is a little better now than it was. Back then it was even worse, and the people could not withstand the taxes. One of the good things I could say, during my tenure, is that I do not think we ever had a tax levy turned down. We only ran them when they were absolutely necessary, and it was always for bare minimum subsistence. But the big problem is that most of your monies in a school district go in labor costs. Let us face it, it is labor intensive and was getting worse and worse. Common sense said to me that at some point you have to realize you are doing the kids an injustice if you cannot, for example, take a vacation. My wife was not very happy, but I never took a vacation during that time because I was scared. In the summertime, I would get so many letters of resignation every day, and then I would have to look for teachers. I was doing that as late as September, up until the last minute. Sometimes it was two months into the school year before I would find someone. I was just literally scared to take a vacation.

Now keep in mind when I took this on, as white headed as I am now, I was 29 years old.[24] There was some advantage to that. I think stress affects you differently, depending on what kind of stress it is. I was an idealist, and I think that kept some of the stress away. I was an idealist and wanted to make something happen. I did a few things that I am proud of. They kind of hang with your memory and make you think it was worthwhile. But common sense prevailed at the point where you say, "Well, look, this thing is getting so bad that it is just not fair to the kids." And I started talking internally with my administrative staff and to other people I knew. Also keep in mind that this was a time period when Democrats were the national leaders. We had a number of Cincinnatians who were reasonably high up, not at the top but reasonably high up in the Justice Department and in the Office of Civil Rights. I was allowed access to those people, once I was through with local talking, to say to them, "Hey, can't something be done about this." I also had some examples around that gave me encouragement. For example, one of the more famous cases was when the Feds went into Chicago and forced them to "integrate," which is questionable. Nevertheless, they got resistance and ul-

timately had to pull all the federal dollars out of Chicago. You can imagine
how many dollars that was. Maybe they got right to the last day they were
going pull the money out, and the politicians said, "Wait a minute, wait a
minute, you asked how many dollars are in between cracks, not just a few
school dollars that flow in for a few school principals but federal dollars."
They had the power to do that. Then you got action. That may have been certainly the biggest, if not the first, situation where that office proved it had
some clout in that regard. Nevertheless, we then began meeting and plotting
(with federal officials, civil rights officials). That is really what happened.

Initially, a man named Allen was my contact in Cincinnati, and he then
brought in the folks from Washington. These are the people I was meeting
with. Of course Allen gave them all the background and laid it all out. And
then they did a little bit of their own investigating. This was an obvious situation, so obvious it didn't take a whole lot to convince folks that, "Gee whiz,
something is wrong here." We then began plotting. The plot was a simple
plot. It was one that said, "Well, let's pull these folk together and start a dialogue." That is always the way to start. They called a meeting and Lucas,
Princeton superintendent, talked about how busy he was. However, he could
not refuse to come when an official, very high on the tree in that office,
called the meeting. After all, this was an unusual situation; it was not like a
local meeting that you would have another chance to attend the next week.
So you get all the superintendents; you get the superintendent from Princeton; you get Wyoming; you get Lockland. Reading may have come to the
first meeting, but I think it was concluded that Reading was not really contiguous with Lincoln Heights. I think Reading breathed a big sigh of relief
and sort of bowed out.

Revoking the Lincoln Heights charter came later.[25] You are way down
the road when you revoke the charter. That comes later. You are no way near
planning what has to happen. The meeting was simply a dialogue for the
Feds to spell out to these other folk what they had found and give them a
chance to refute it. Most of them knew that they could not refute it, so they
just sat silently and seemed to say, "What do you do next?" We may have
had two or three of those kinds of meetings with the agenda being established each time for the next one. But from there, the same group, meaning
myself and the Feds, went to the state because the state has a role to play
here in Ohio. As a matter of fact, under the constitution, states have total responsibility for education and its configuration. The research had been done;

therefore the state superintendent was called upon to interact. You knew that if he so desired he could stir up this pot. But, as I told you earlier, he had just come out of a fight that he was not about to go into again. There was a Black school district called Spencer, very much like Lincoln Heights, that he and the state school board summarily annexed to Toledo. Spencer did not want to be annexed, so that turned out to be a dogfight. Now it is like anything else when people are resistant, you get all kinds of fights. You got dirty, and his—the state superintendent's—name got muddy. The fight was Black/White; it was economic; it was all kinds of things. Most people in most jobs do not mind a challenge, but they like for it to be kind of smooth and not too many waves. Anyway, the state superintendent was nearing the end of his tenure. He had gotten bloody in the Spencer fight, and he was not about to come in here and declare what he was going to do, particularly with this group of fairly sophisticated, fairly politically savvy (in terms of whom they knew) folk. So he sort of resisted and the Feds had to threaten him. They said (I am paraphrasing), "Whether you like it or not, you have a role to play by law. You are going to have to play the role or maybe we will have to look at the whole state of Ohio." Well, he thought, "God, what do I do now?" One of his assistant superintendents not only recognized the handwriting on the wall but was very proactive. He realized that redistricting was long over-due, and it was "misdone" in the first place. He became our state angel be-cause he was very supportive of us during the time of the merger. He tried his best to convince the state superintendent to take the initiative and to take some steps toward remedying the situation. What the superintendent finally said was, "Okay, we defined the section of law that brings the state into play here. I am going to assign this to you and you execute it." It was really like saying, "I will have a fall guy if it all falls through." He protected himself against being totally out front, but as it turned out, much to his amazement, in the end he, the state superintendent, could put a feather in his cap.

1968/69 was the exact period that this was going on. Once the assistant state superintendent received that assignment, there were meetings between state officials and this local group of superintendents.[26] The superintendents then realized, "Hey, we not only have the Feds on our back, but we are not going to get much help from the state." So little by little the water was rising and there was no land in sight. Because of the way the situation was unfold-ing, there was this feeling that somebody was going to drown. Following four or five meetings, we got to what looked like "decision time," "put up or answer" kind of time. Bob Lucas, Princeton Superintendent, was smart enough to realize this. You aim at Princeton in the first place because that is where Lincoln Heights should have been in the very beginning. But what scared Lockland to death was the fact that we, Lincoln Heights, had more people and more students than Lockland. That was all they wanted, I'm being sarcastic, was to merge with us and we just take over their school district making the Black/White ratio at least 60/40. They were scared to death.

Wyoming was just a little bit scared because it owned this tiny bit of land down here near the railroad track that was contiguous, just a little strip of land. The superintendent, quickly on behalf of his board, said, "You can have this." He got his board to work that in. It was not worth mentioning. It was just a little strip of land you could do nothing with. It was on this side, down by the railroad tracks. Wyoming quickly said, "That's all we have to give." They basically said, "We are a poor school district anyway." And technically, it is poor from the standpoint of taxes.[27] It pays for its schools. Most schools were supported largely by industry and supplemented by homeowners, whereas Wyoming paid for its schools.

Lockland is a similar case. For many years, when Lockland was obviously rich, it was the number one or number two lowest tax district in the state of Ohio. The per-capita number of students versus the income from business was very high. That just changed recently. I can remember when I was superintendent (just a bit of an aside), I would welcome anything given to me and then decide whether I could use it or not. Lockland would give me new books they had bought. Sometimes we could use them and sometimes we could not. But these books had not been taken out of the box. They could afford it; money was nothing to them; they were rich per capita. They were scared that money was going to come to them, and they would be in charge of Lincoln Heights' Blacks. So Bob Lucas worked a sideline deal that never came to the front until the final meeting. His sideline deal was to frighten the Lockland superintendent. It scared him to death. Lucas suggested, "Well, what we've got to do is divvy up the Lincoln Heights students. I will take half and you take half. (Like a piece of meat.) We will draw up maps." Well, even half was overwhelming to Lockland. There was and always has been this racial animosity. People are taught by politicians to hate each other because that is part of the political control process. The history of animosity between Lincoln Heights and Lockland is tremendous. What is interesting is that if you go back to the 1930s, most of the kids in Lincoln Heights went to

Lockland High School, not just Lockland Wayne after they built it, but Lockland High School. They have Black pictures on the wall.

But anyway, Lockland did not want those Black kids. Lucas convinced them saying, "Well, if we have to take them then you have to give us some money." That is how that $35,000,000 worth of duplicate came up.[28] When they had the last meeting of this type, Bob came in and sort of officially announced that they would do it—merge with Lincoln Heights. I do not remember the exact words but they all meant the same thing. He announced that Lockland had agreed that they would contribute $35,000,000 in tax duplicates. That was like taking that inventory that was initially shifted from Lincoln Heights over to Lockland, back over to Princeton. That was all it meant. It was the craziest thing you have ever seen, if you can laugh at it in retrospect, but it was really serious business. They shifted the inventory on paper. Anyway, that is how they got the $35,000,000 in duplicate. And from that point on it was a matter of, "Okay, when and how do we make it happen?"

Again, there was never an option of transferring money to Lincoln Heights.[29] Personally, (I say "personally" because I don't want to mislead you about anybody else), I certainly would have thought twice if that kind of offer would have been on the table. I am not saying where I would have settled, but I would have thought twice. First of all, I would have had to define that offer. For example, I may have said, "Okay, I want GE—the General Electric Plant—back, lock, stock, and barrel." I do not think they were about to do that but that option was never made available. You would have to ask for something that was stable enough to go for the long haul, not just a fixed amount of money, such as a few million dollars, for a one-shot deal. I would have asked for GE because it was growing big then. (Of course, it is going down now and I would be hurting now.) They had a peak of 12,000–13,000 workers, and between the plant itself and a 1% or 2% salary tax, you could do pretty good. You would do very well, as a matter of fact, for a small district. Now that brings into to play all the reasons why I would have accepted that. I would have accepted the offer of GE because I have never been in favor of political integration. Political integration is when you bring mostly poor Blacks and Whites together. This is because in the early days of so-called integration, they moved poor people around, for the most part. Non-poor people were able to outmaneuver integration and, in addition, they were making decisions in the end. A few middle-class people were involved in bussing, and in some few liberal communities you may have seen what you think of as pure integration. But I do not know of any schools that had pure integration because it went from segregated to politically integrated. In other words, you brought the groups together, and then you went to internal segregation within the schools. Tracking, for example. I was never in favor of that, and I sometimes regret that I did not have the propensity to write my opinions on the matter. I see so much writing on the subject now that I say, "Boy, I said that thirty years ago." Now the impact of political integration versus pure integration is becoming obvious.

To Cincinnati Public Schools

After the merger was solidified, I went to Cincinnati Public Schools. I had the choice of remaining with the Princeton district as Bob Lucas's assistant or going to Cincinnati as an assistant. I chose to go to Cincinnati for two reasons. First of all, my interest was in the kind of young people that were being left behind in cities as families migrated to the suburbs. And Princeton, of course, historically has been a middle-class district although it now has flattened out somewhat because of the altered Black/White ratio or in terms of the increased numbers of low-income and/or Black students. I felt I would be more comfortable working with the kids who were being left behind because I felt like I was a natural advocate. That is why I went to Cincinnati. And, of course, it was also timely that a job opportunity opened up. Actually my wife was responsible for me taking that job, to be honest with you, because she was teaching in Cincinnati at the time. She came home one day with an application, and said, "Here, they're going to hire...."

Lawrence Hawkins has since retired from the University of Cincinnati as a vice president, but he was the first Black assistant superintendent in Cincinnati. He had made a decision to leave the school system and go to the university, and they were looking for a replacement. The question was whether they were going to recruit from within or without. Cincinnati had a history of not hiring anybody from outside of the system to fill positions below the superintendency. This policy had led to dogfights among the staff for promotions. My wife went on to say, "You're the best qualified; you ought to apply for this job." I laughed about it and said, "No, I've got a job. I am negotiating with Bob Lucas up here. I know we're going to fight like dogs, Bob and I, but I probably will be representative of the Black folk—that is the way it will turn out."

Paul Miller, the superintendent of Cincinnati at the time, and I were friends because we both went to the same meetings and belonged to the same professional organizations. We saw each other frequently. I saw him in Columbus one day, we were standing there talking in the back of a meeting against the wall. I said, "Hey Paul, I might be interested in that job." And he said...he had a nickname for me, he called me Hollis Willoway, which is reversing my name. He said, "Write me a letter and tell me you are formally interested." I said, "I might do that." So I wrote him a one-paragraph letter, with no detail, and just said I would be interested in that job, but I told him, not in the letter but personally, that I was not going through all the hassle that goes on down there. These were Black folks going through this hassle because it was going to be a job given to a Black person. All the people near that level were vying for this job. It would have been the second Black person to be hired at that level and the only Black person in the cabinet. I told Paul that I was not going through all the hassle because I really did not need a job that badly. To my surprise, he called me back later and said he wanted to send a couple of people out to talk to me. He sent a couple of his assistants out to talk.

Actually, I was shocked that they hired me. Having been "free" in Lincoln Heights—I use that expression because that's significant—to operate differently, I could not behave like the folk who were internal and had been trained by the system here. However, I told them the reasons why I thought they needed a person like me. They had a rule that you had to live in the city if you held a job at that level. I said, "I'm not moving." They made a dispensation. They took a good report back, and I then had to meet with the board. That surprised me.

I went to meet and have dinner with the board of education. I tried to talk myself out of a job you might say. I didn't try, it just happened that way, because basically I shared with them the changing demographics in the city, which were obvious if you paid much attention. The Black/White ratio was changing fast, and the Cincinnati district was moving more towards fifty-fifty. "You need a person like me because one thing I will do instinctively is tell you the truth. Now you may not agree with me, but I'm going to tell you the truth. And the truth means that the superintendent, whoever it happens to be, or the board may not like it all the time. But it will be an honest truth in terms of how you deal with this new emerging district differently from how you dealt with the old district." The old district was dealt with very typically as school districts have been operating in this country, for that matter. And that is to say, that at the policy-making level you had basically White, middle-class people making policy decisions and had little or no understanding of the emerging and growing number of poor kids and how to treat them. So they treat them like they treat the other kids. That doesn't work. I just stated that simply and short enough. There are a few that get through, but it kills off a great many others. To me, this ratio means that the system does not work. In other words, there are a few people who get by, and they brag about the fact that, "Well, I did it." But at the time they do not think about all the folk who died along the way, even though a few made it. So I said, "You know, I'm going to tell you. I am not going to let you make policy while I am sitting there, being the highest-paid Black, and say nothing. I may not have enough votes to change it so I will be a voice in the wilderness." To my surprise, they offered me the job. That landed me in Cincinnati and turned out to be an excellent decision for many reasons. It benefited me personally, and at the same time it also allowed me to promote Ed Starr to Bob Lucas. He had the opportunity to move from high school principal to become the first Black assistant superintendent in Princeton. My decision to go to Cincinnati created more jobs, you might say, in that regard. I went to Cincinnati late in 1970. This was after the 1968/69 academic year in which all the negotiations took place that ultimately led to the Princeton merger.

Eddie Lawrence Starr
Principal, Lincoln Heights High School, 1963–1970
Associate Principal, Princeton High School, 1970–1972
Associate Superintendent, Princeton School District, 1972–1996

Educational Background

I was born in Lincoln Heights on Steffens Street two doors down from where the police station is now. I guess we moved to what is now Evandale when I was maybe one year old or so.[30] I went to St. Simon's School for the kindergarten, first and second grades. Because I was too young, the public schools wouldn't take me at that time. I wasn't five in September—I was born in October—but I was able to get into the kindergarten at St. Simon's.[31] So my mother would bring me over everyday from Evandale to go. When I was promoted into the third grade I went to the Evandale public school. They had a school there from kindergarten through eighth grade. I finished the eighth grade there in 1945.

The Black families in Evandale lived there on the property of Tennessee Corporation Fertilizer Factory. They had three duplexes on the property, and Black families lived in them. There were three, three-room, shotgun buildings where six families lived. The parents worked in the fertilizer factory, so we had free rent, free everything, free water, but the facilities weren't that great. We didn't have inside plumbing, and we had to go outside and get the water and that whole bit, which was not unusual during that time. Even in Lincoln Heights there were people who had water but other people had to get water. They would buy water from people by the bucketful to carry back to their homes. Every house didn't have water. In 1945 when I graduated from the eighth grade from Evandale Elementary, I could have gone to any high school in Greater Cincinnati, and they, Evandale, would have paid my tuition. But we had friends in Lockland, and I had grown up knowing people who went to Lockland Wayne High School. They had a great basketball team, and I used to follow them around, so I chose to go to Lockland Wayne.

Lockland Wayne was all Black. It was the segregated school in Lockland. The history of Lockland is a little funny. At one time the Lockland School District had been integrated, and the Black kids from down there in Lincoln Heights (I don't know exactly where the cut-off was) from Jackson Street along Lockland Road all went to East Lockland. But in the '40s someone decided that the Blacks would be more comfortable in their own school, so they built Lockland Wayne. They had an elementary and high school. The kids from Lincoln Heights went there. Now I don't know whether Lincoln Heights ever had to pay them tuition for their kids to go on or not. There might have been a trade-off because Lockland needed bodies in order to run the high school. Most of the students in Lockland Wayne High School were from Lincoln Heights. So that is where I went. I graduated from Lockland Wayne in 1949, and I went to Miami University in Oxford, Ohio. I graduated from there with a B.A. in 1953 with a sociology major and psychology minor.

I was drafted, and I spent two years in the army—from 1953 to 1955—with one year in Korea. I was an enlisted man and made the rank of specialist III, which was equivalent to a corporal. I didn't want to go to OCS, Officer's Candidate School. I guess 95% of my training group were college graduates because they got us in November. If you finish your basic training and you go to OCS, you come out a second lieutenant. They could get very few people to go to OCS because if you ended up as an officer and happened to get into the infantry during the Korean Conflict, your life expectancy wasn't very long. There were a number of other reasons. One, as a commissioned officer, we were told that we could be called back in the service at any time because we were commissioned officers. If you were non-com, once you finished your reserve time, it would take an act of Congress, an act of war to bring you back in. So I made the decision that I wanted to go in, spend my two years, and get out. So that is what happened.

Prior to going in the service I had said I wanted be a psychiatric social worker, and I wanted to go to the University of Pittsburgh's social work school. I had already had three deferments at Miami, so they wouldn't give me another one. I came back and decided I wanted to teach. I used the GI bill to go to Xavier University here in Cincinnati to work on English and social studies as teaching fields and got a masters degree in guidance and counseling.

From Teacher to Principal

I finished my masters around 1958, and that is the time I went to St. Simon's to teach the eighth grade—the self-contained eighth grade class.[32] I stayed there two years; then I went to Lincoln Heights High School as a social studies teacher in 1960.

When I left Xavier I had teaching certifications in social studies and in English. I had a lot more hours in social studies than in English. Because I was in a liberal arts program in Miami, I had sociology, psychology, and history. When I pulled all that together it gave me a comprehensive social studies concentration and English. I never worked as a guidance counselor even though I had my masters in guidance and counseling. There was no opening for a guidance counselor at Lincoln Heights. There was only one such position, and they already had a guidance counselor but there was an opening for a teacher.

I taught world history, world geography, and American history, but I never taught English as a subject. I made my kids angry with me because I also taught English throughout these other subjects. I said, "You have to write." I forced them to write. They didn't have these one-word answer tests. I wanted a narrative, and they had to know how to spell because I would take off for spelling. They learned how to do that.

I had always wanted to teach high school,[33] and at the time Cincinnati was not hiring Black high school teachers readily. They were hiring Blacks in elementary school but if you wanted to teach high school, you either had to teach at Lincoln Heights, Lockland Wayne was still in existence at that time, or Lincoln Grant in Covington—Covington's all-Black school. You could teach at a place like Dayton Dunbar, an all-Black school in Dayton, and other places around the country like Charleston, West Virginia—they had Garnet High School there. There was a high school in Indianapolis, where Oscar Robinson attended—Chrispus Attucks—that was all-Black. Those are the places that we could teach high school. The other folks really weren't hiring Blacks in high school and very few in elementary. It turned out to be an advantage for us at Lincoln Heights High School to get good teachers because if you wanted to teach high school, you couldn't go any-where else. We got good teachers even though we were not paying a lot of money. We were able to get good teachers for a few years. In the late 60s we started to have trouble keeping our teachers because Cincinnati started hiring Black teachers on the secondary level.

Eventually it became difficult to find teachers and Cincinnati had to open up some.[34] There was always a pressure by the NAACP and other groups in these big school districts about hiring more Blacks. So with the number of Black kids that Cincinnati had, it was just a matter of time that they had to start to honor that. We'd get our teachers from our recruiting in the South. We'd bring them up and they would stay with us a couple of years, and they would move on to Cincinnati.[35]

So you see, it became very difficult for us. Let me put this in some type of time frame. I taught at Lincoln Heights for two years—from '60 to '62. I left Lincoln Heights for one year, and I worked at Hamilton County Court House in the Court of Domestic Relations because we had trouble the year before with our salaries. The rumor was that we were going to get a reduc-tion in pay that next year, the '62/'63 school year. I said, "I just can't afford to do that." The job came open in the Court of Domestic Relations, which was in the area of social work. I had always said that I wanted to do that kind of work. I said, "I want to try this." I worked there for one year but in 1963, I went back to Lincoln Heights as a high school principal.

Holloway held that job open for me for one year. When I went to the Court of Domestic Relations, that July he told me they had made him admin-istrative head, superintendent. He asked me if I would consider taking the principalship. Well, I had promised Judge Paul George that I would stay at least a year because he had said, "You are coming out of education and I don't want this to be a summer job situation once we start to train you." I said, "I will be here at least a year," and he agreed. That was in June. Holloway came down the last of July after he got promoted from principal of the high school. He asked me if I would take the high school principalship. That was the thing I wanted more than anything. I wanted to be a high school principal because I felt that I could bring some things to the kids and the staff. But I told him that I promised the judge that I was going to stay a year, and I wasn't going to go back on that promise. So he convinced the board, I guess, to hold the position open. That next year, Holloway came around the last part of June or the first part of July and asked me if I felt that I had fulfilled my obligation. I said that I was ready to go. I was high school principal from 1963 to 1970. Now, the first four years there, 1963 to 1967/68, we didn't have a problem getting good qualified people at the high school.

Teaching before the Merger

You see, no one, including us—I am speaking of the Lincoln Heights staff—were sure what kind of job we were doing. We knew we were working like heck. We had worked hard with those kids. We had developed pretty self-sufficient youngsters, and the caliber of youngsters that we sent to them helped the merger. We didn't send them little "fraidy-like" kids. Our kids were pretty aggressive and pretty self-assured about how to conduct themselves. Those were the things that I started to work on from day one, from the time I went in Lincoln Heights High School as a teacher. The year before I was told that the kids were swinging off things, and it was like *Blackboard Jungle*.

Holloway became principal in 1960 I think. He approached me about coming down to teach, and he recruited several other men. We came into that building and brought some discipline. We had to get some discipline right away. We always felt that without good discipline you can't teach very effectively. So that was the first emphasis—you had to know how to act. I said, "If you are going to be here, there are certain ways you are going to act in this building. Now I can't control what you do out there; I prefer that you act the same way out there, but once you come into this building, this is the way it is going to be." And we had to make it stick.

Holloway was also a very innovative kind of administrator for the times, and he made us do some things as a staff that at first I didn't want to do. One of the things he said was, "You must go out and visit the students in your homeroom." We were to visit them at their houses, in the evenings, at the very beginning of the school year. And he didn't want it dragged out. I had from 25 to 30 kids in my homeroom. "Oh, I don't want to do that," but I went out there, sat down, and started talking to these parents. We had a rapport and I found myself having to tear myself away and say, "Look I've got to get to somewhere else." They would start, "Let me tell you something, you just let me know if that guy or that girl…does something wrong." This was the best thing we ever did because the parents got to know us. At that time parents weren't afraid to be parents. They were parents; they would put hands on and that helped us a great deal. Over the years, we maintained this practice. Every year that we were there, operating as a Lincoln Heights School District, that was one of the things the new teachers had to do. They had to go in and visit those parents. They had to sit down and talk to them and let them know what we expected and what we were trying to do.

Later we started to get scholarship money to help kids into college, and that was a bigger selling point. If the parents would do what we were asking them to do, they would have an opportunity to get this money; it would help the kids get scholarships. I'm skipping over giving you a big overview here. One of the big things that would happen at our graduation was when we would read off the kids' names that were going to college and the scholarship money that they would receive. Then I would multiply the amount by four. But really if they stayed in the program, they would get that or more. This got the attention of the parents and it got their support. We got their support so that was very helpful.

When we lost a chemistry teacher who had been there for years, I could not find a competent chemistry teacher. I ended up hiring a Chinese woman who had not had the background around Blacks, and the kids just beat her down. We knew that we were weak in these areas of math and science. But there was one thing that helped us and surprised a lot of people. In talking with General Electric and Ford and others, Holloway convinced them to send people over to work with our kids after school. These men from the plants would be in there working with our college-prep kids on chemistry, physics, and math. This was something that did not show up on paper. We couldn't carry these people as teachers, nor could you report what they were doing as part of your curriculum, but they were teaching our kids the science and the math they needed to know. They volunteered. We told them what we needed. There are always people out there like that, who are willing to help if you indicate that you need help. They got to know our kids, and the kids were receptive to folks coming in. That was very helpful to us.

There were other things that we did. We knew that everybody wasn't going to college. We were able to get an outstanding business teacher, Mrs. Morris, who came in from General Electric. She had been a secretary at General Electric, and she got into our business program. Her specialty was shorthand and typing. She pushed those girls, and every year I would have several explosions down there. "I can't take it." They thought she was too hard. They'd come down to the office; I would listen to them; we'd work it out, and I'd send them back.

We also arranged to have our girls go over and take the exams that GE would give to people who were applying for jobs. They kept failing. We said, "Well what is the problem?" Helen went over and sat down with the people there at GE, and they analyzed what was happening. Well, the kids could take the dictation and they could type, but they were having trouble with the spelling and grammar—grammatical structure. So we came back, and for that group we added the best English teacher to do extra work with them. They started passing these exams. We had a strong group of girls who went out and worked in the secretarial areas.

We knew that one of the things that kids didn't have when they left high school and went looking for jobs was work experience. They never had work experience. It took a long time for Holloway to work through the details, but cooperating industries gave us some job slots. We would release kids who had at least C averages for a quarter term. It turned out that these students were seniors. They would go to work every day just as if they were out of school. They would go to work, report to their supervisors, and do what they were asked to do. We also set it up so that they would come back two nights a week to turn in homework, pick up the work that the teachers had for them, and get the help they might need. This kept their grades up but we had to have fairly good students to begin with. This arrangement would end up doing a couple of things for poor kids. One, they made some spending money, and, two, it gave them a work experience. It gave them a feel for what they had to do on that job to be successful.

Before the merger we knew that we were going into the Princeton District the spring of 1970. We knew that in the fall. The only thing that we really changed was the fact that I told the students, "You are going into the Princeton District and I think you are going to do okay."[36] But we had been talking all those years about how we act. When I first went to Lincoln Heights as teacher and principal they would not allow us to join the Hamilton County Athletic League. We were a county school, but we could not play basketball or football in the league. The excuse was that "Well, Black kids fight." They didn't come out publicly and shout it, but this was what it was all about. For those schools that did play us, we had to make sure that we didn't have problems. I would talk to the kids before a game. If there were two buses, I would be on the first one and had other staff members with us. We would patrol those stadiums and places. I'd talk to our kids and say, "We'll cheer hard. When they come into our building we want it to be like a snake pit but with good clean things. I don't want to hear any profanity or any disrespectful cheers or anything." I would walk my little sidelines, and they knew that if I found someone who wasn't being respectful, they would come out of there. We were small enough for me to say, for instance, "Pat, didn't I put you out last week?" "Yes, sir." "Well why are you here?" Because my thing was, "You're out until you can come in and say to me I know what it means to be a Lincoln Heights Tiger. I know I can control myself." I would then say, "So, okay, you're sure you can handle it?" "Yes sir." "Okay, you are reinstated." That's the way we did it. And we cheered, cheered, cheered but always very respectful.

The Merger

Princeton fought tooth and nail to keep us from being merged; however, to their credit, to the Board of Education and to Dr. Lucas's credit, once it was determined that that merger was going to take place, they did everything they could to make it work. I remember in a meeting, Dr. Lucas just laid it out. There were staff members for it, and there were staff members against it and a lot of White staff members who had never been around Blacks. They had a few Blacks there from Glendale and from Woodlawn, but they were afraid of the Lincoln Heights Blacks coming in. And even some of the Black parents from those other areas were afraid of what the influx of Blacks kids from Lincoln Heights would do to their situation. "We thought we left you folks behind, now here you come up in here."[37] That is one reason they were concerned. But, in looking back, it only made it better for them. There were Whites and Blacks against it. But there were Whites for it and there were Blacks for it. As an administrator, I was for it. I didn't even know what our future was going to be, but we had gotten to the point where it was harder to get teachers.

I think that the strong stand that Dr. Lucas took after the merger really helped. He was in one of the first general meetings. He said, "I only think it is right that we take these kids from Lincoln Heights in and try to give them the best education that we can give them, and anyone who doesn't feel that way I think it is time for you to start looking for somewhere else to go." That is what he said. And some people left. And some people stayed who really would have liked to go.

The role I played in the merger[38] was that of the school administrator. They weren't sure whether the students at Lincoln Heights could handle the curriculum at Princeton. I was not privy to the discussions concerning whether or not we felt our kids could handle the work. So the decision was made and this was a decision made for us. It was decided that the best thing to do was to allow the students who were graduating from the eighth grade at the time of the merger, who were going into the ninth grade, to immediately go to Princeton. The students who were in the tenth, eleventh, and twelfth grades would remain at Lincoln Heights because they weren't sure whether or not the students could handle their level of academics. My role was to make sure that the curricula were coordinated and that what we were teaching at Lincoln Heights would be what they would have been taught at Princeton. (After the merger, we referred to the two facilities as the north campus and the south campus.) Then I asked the superintendent what opportunities would students have to choose courses at the main campus. He said there would be no problem if Lincoln Heights' students wanted to take courses up there. We did have a pretty good number of students electing to take courses at the main campus. At each period change we had a bus waiting to load up kids there at the south campus, and a bus would load up at the north campus and our kids would go back and forth based on the classes they took. Some of the kids would stay up there for two or three periods, taking courses at the main campus that we might not have had at the south campus. Well, the kids did pretty good, so the next year they decided that there was no reason to keep them separated, and they moved everything up to the main campus.

Space was not the reason that the tenth, eleventh, and twelve grades of former Lincoln Heights students initially stayed at the south campus.[39] Well, we did have a space problem, but the space problem was solved in this sense; we ended up having two buildings for the ninth graders. At the time they had a building in Woodlawn that existed before the original merger.[40] It wasn't a high school building but a big elementary building. What we did was split the ninth grade up. Part of the ninth grade went to that Woodlawn building, and the other part of the ninth grade went to the old Lincoln Heights building, what they called the south campus. And at the main campus you had the tenth, eleventh, and twelfth grades. That is how we solved the space problem. I can't remember exactly which years we set those two buildings up. That did not start until the second year or might have been down in our third or fourth year, but we did go to an overlap[41] for a period of time also. Oh no, they won't say that they were afraid Lincoln Heights students would not be able to handle the curriculum, but that is what it really was.

So at the time of the merger the Lincoln Heights class club presidents and officers, since their freshmen and sophomore years, had directed their money-making projects toward giving the seniors their prom—giving the junior/senior prom. The junior class was supposed to finance that. So each year I would give them a report at the beginning of the year of what they had in their class club and how much money they had. Then they would develop projects, and we would approve the money-making projects that they would have for the year. So they were accustomed to doing that. Well, when we got ready to go to Princeton, I was concerned. Now you always think the other people on the other side are doing much better than you are. I assumed that they would have much more money in their treasury than we had in ours, but I wanted to make sure that our kids had a say in what went on. So I called the presidents in and said, "You know we are going into Princeton next year; you've got 'x' number of dollars here. What I am going to do is to let you spend a hundred dollars of your money for whatever you want to do with your class. But the rest of the money, I feel we should send up to your class club treasury." And they all agreed to that. I explained that when they are having a class club meeting at Princeton, "I don't want you to feel that you can't talk, and you don't have the right to speak up." Well, it turned out that we had more money than they had.

So I found out that the money we had sent was more money than the Princeton seniors had, and they had hundreds more kids than we had. I told our kids, "You had 'x' amount of dollars in there, and this is what they have, so don't you feel that you have to take a back seat when you talk about class plans and everything. You don't have to take a back seat to anybody. Your money is there." I didn't have to tell them that because I had some strong people in there like Annette Harding. She is a doctor now.

We sent up a nice bunch of kids, and they were able to take care of themselves and hold their own pretty well. They knew how to organize their clubs and that kind of thing, so it went pretty well for them. But the first few years, we had two valedictorians; an old Princeton valedictorian and a new Princeton valedictorian from Lincoln Heights. Annette Harding was a valedictorian based on her test scores and things from Lincoln Heights. And for a while we ran two kings and queens to make sure that the Blacks kids were able to get involved in everything. We stopped doing that after the kids were familiar with one another. They've since had a number of Black class presidents, kings, and queens elected from the general student body.

Let me step back one step. My title that first year was associate principal. Ohio State had done a study on administrative organization, and they had made a recommendation to the Princeton district that it set up an administrative structure that would have an associate superintendent, an associate principal at the high school, an associate principal at the junior school along with the principal and assistant principals. The associate was to take a lot of the pressure off the principal and would be doing a lot more hands-on things. They felt that with buildings as big as the high school, there were a lot of other things that the principal would be involved in versus hands-on, day-to-day operation of the building—that fell into the associate principal's hands. So I was an associate principal when I was in another building—when I was at the south campus in Lincoln Heights. The second year, when we moved up to the main campus, I moved my office there, and I became the associate at the high school and worked very closely with the high school principal.

I think I had four assistant principals at that time, one at each grade level. You see, my position was what I made it but was influenced by the situation. The principal at the time I went there was Don Johnson. Dr Johnson, a very learned man, did not like any kind of confrontation or pressure. So he was very happy to let me do the things that needed to be done sometimes in working with staff and talking with people. For instance, I came into the building one morning, and one of the industrial arts teachers was reprimanding a Black kid. I came in the back, and seniors had their lockers along this area. This teacher said, "Now you go back down there." He wanted the student to go back down to the corner "and walk back up here." All these kids were standing along the way. I said to the teacher, "What happened here?" He said, "Oh, he was running down the hall, and I told him to stop." I said, "Well, did he stop when you told him?" He said, "Yes, he stopped and I told him to go back down there." And I said, "You don't really expect for him to do that, do you?" "Yes, why not?" I said, "You've got this kid out here in front of his friends, peers and people, and you are treating him like he were a kindergartener or something. This is a senior and he is going to give us a problem." And that is what he was doing. "Well," I said, "Son, get your stuff and go to class." I got his name so that I could get to him later on. "Go to class." The teacher said, "Well, we are going to see Johnson about this." I said, "Yes, let's go see Dr. Johnson." He went in and he said what he had to say. I said that I came upon the situation and told what I did. "I could see that kid afterwards, but he was going to cause a problem and we don't need that." Johnson didn't want to say anything. He said, "Well, you go ahead and work it out." The teacher was mad, but it was those kind of things that took place.

Now John Hillard was an assistant principal. He was Black, and we had some other strong teachers who were able to help White teachers understand. We had a lot of meetings about how we were to deal with the students. A lot of them were anticipating problems that didn't happen. First thing, the Black kids were pretty mannerable with adults. The kids today aren't, but at that time it was "yes Sir, yes, Ma'am" from the Black kids. They respected adult authority. So if you didn't push them the wrong way, they would pretty well go along with the situation. We would always say, even at Lincoln Heights, "You don't fight that fight with that teacher. If that teacher and you don't agree then you shut your mouth, and then you come down here and say, 'I've got a concern and this happened' and we can work it out. But if you stand up there and start yelling and carrying on and that teacher throws you out, I have no other recourse except to deal with you as an unruly student even though what you say might have some merit. But you don't take on that teacher in that classroom. You've got to learn how to go through the procedure for doing that."

Johnson didn't like a lot of things on him, and so this associateship was developed as we went along. I said, "Hey, I'm the associate, so you guys (the assistant principals) report to me." Whether they wanted to or not, it was to Johnson's advantage to have them report to me. I handled most of the problems, and usually I would go in, sit down, and tell him what was going on and what I wanted to do. Sometimes I wouldn't do anything until I had talked to him. He was the final decision maker, and he had the right to know these things. So we made a good team. He got to where he trusted me, and I understood what he wanted and how he wanted some things. But sometimes I felt that we needed to do something different, and I would go in and explain to him why I thought so.

For instance, one of the big things was Black history. The Princeton teachers did not embrace Black history month with a lot of enthusiasm, and I was saying why we needed it. At that time we had more Black staff than they ever had before, and we had some competent Black staff members. Once I got through the staff, I had to go to the board. During that time there was a lady on the board from Sharonville, and she didn't like the merger. I would go in and present the program for Black history month and had to fight her all the way, all the time. She'd ask a lot of questions and I'd try to give the answers. We'd go at it. But eventually she became president of the board, and she started to learn some things and she became a very strong president. She wasn't the racist person that I thought she was starting out, and she did a good job. So yes, she would give me problems, but then it got to the point where she became very supportive.

I moved to associate superintendent in 1972. They had never filled that job. Even though they had set the associate up at the high school and the junior high school, they had never filled that post at the superintendent level. So they opened that job up. I did not apply for the job; I just assumed that a Black guy who had been in the district the longest was going to get it. One day Dr. Lucas came over and I was out in the hallway at lunchtime, because I would be out in the hall and I would talk with kids. He said, "Mr. Starr, I would like to talk to you a little bit." I said, "Well, Dr. Lucas, I'm on duty right now but as soon as lunch is over..." So he stood there for a while and I was speaking to kids. "Hey, that's a pretty dress," I would say, and kids would come up and ask me questions. But they didn't know Dr. Johnson, so Dr. Lucas said, "So how do you get to know so many kids?" I said, "I'm out here every day." I said, "Dr. Lucas, the same kids come by here at the same time almost everyday. And sometimes, I'd say, 'you know I forgot your name' or just say pleasant things to them, 'how things are going...' Black and White kids..." We went in and he told me that they had interviewed several people for the job, but he just felt that every time he talked to me all I would talk about was my kids. Then he told me he would like to offer me the job. He said, "But Dr. Johnson said you didn't want it. You didn't want to leave." I said, "Dr. Lucas, this is a great job as the associate. When I was scheduling down at Lincoln Heights, I only had about fourteen rooms or so and had all those single-offered courses. Up here you have all this room; you have multiple offerings; I have a computer man at my beck and call—I tell him what I want and he does it." And I said, "I really love it but I would love the challenge of the other job too." And so, of course I had to say, "I need to talk this over with my wife."

Well I already knew what I was going to do. My wife was at RELIS, Robert E. Lucas Intermediate School,[42] and I called and had the principal go in and get her. She was a team leader there. I said, "Now don't shout or holler or do anything that people could recognize, but you are talking to the next associate superintendent of Princeton School District." She said, "What did you say?" I said, "Of course, I couldn't make a decision until I talked it over with my wife." So she was the one who caught hell because teachers always thought that she knew more than she knew. We were in salary negotiations, and they'd ask, "What is he saying? What is he going to do?" She'd say, "I don't know; he won't tell me anything." The teachers were always worried when they were talking around her. They didn't want to talk too much because they thought she'd bring it back to me.

I enjoyed the superintendency as much as the principalship. It was different. It was like going from the classroom to the principalship. In the classroom I had an opportunity to influence a lot of kids, and I was the big guy in there. But as the principal, I not only had an opportunity to influence the kids but also the staff that taught the kids, which is very important to me. The most important job of a principal, of any administrator as I see it, is that of staff development. You've got to help that staff become as effective in doing what they are supposed to do as they possibly can. Part of that is making sure that they are prepared academically and are able to really teach what they know. I would tell teachers "If you are failing so many students, then you have to look at yourself because there's something that you are not doing. Because if you are teaching, they should not be failing; they should be absorbing something here. So, don't tell me how bad they are; you've got to do something here to turn this thing around. Because if you've got a high percentage of failures, don't look at that as being student failures but as a failure on your part to reach some of your students. Now I am not saying that it is all your fault but that you've got to be looking into this. You just can't write it off and say, well they are not studying. You've got to deal with that." I have always felt that is part of it.

I also dealt with the principals. I always wanted the Black administrators to be part of our team, and I wanted to be with them on that team. And I didn't want to be a dictator, and it bothered me when I had someone I had to direct all the time versus "Here is the big picture and here is what we want to do. There are a lot of different ways of reaching our goals within the big picture that are within our guidelines." They had to be able to get out there and function. All I wanted them to do if they had a problem, or thought they had a problem, was to let me know, and then we would work on the problem. Otherwise, "Run your building." And if that's within the guidelines, we meet every week, and we talk about where we want to go and what we're doing. We talk about their problems or if a person has a problem in one building and someone else has had a solution to it, we wanted them to share it. "Don't keep it to yourself. If you have something good, share it. This is a team. If Harry is great over there, and Henry is having a problem, why wouldn't we want to help Henry? If you have an answer to something, or you have a technique or you know something that he should know, share it." I always told them, "I am never going to let you make a fool out of yourself if I know better, and I would expect you not to allow me to do that if you know something. Now if I'm sitting here telling you something and you know very well that, wherever it is, something is wrong, and you sit there and let me go through all this and put me out there, I have a problem with that. I want you to view me as part of the team too. I'm evaluating you, but we always set up our evaluations so that we would identify the weaknesses."

One of the things I did was to develop an evaluation procedure that included teachers. Administrators didn't like that too well. I had a long list of things; it was a Likert five-scale. Now there were always those who felt that the principal walked on water, and others felt that he was terrible in certain areas, but once I went through the whole staff the majority of the people would give a pretty solid evaluation of him. We'd pull all that information together, and that person could see his or her weaknesses as perceived by others. The perception may or may not be accurate, but if they perceive it that way, what is that telling us? We need to look at it and do something about it. Either they're not understanding all this good stuff you're doing, or we're not doing enough good stuff. We would have them create some objectives in order to change the perception. Over a period of time you could see that people would get a better score on certain weaknesses they had worked on.

I would have to look at the overall picture. I would do the same with the teachers and with the central administrators who had input into the building and everything. We had a chance to look at a person from the eyes of many different people along with my personal observations. We were then able to sit down and say, "Here is something concrete that you can look at." Most strong administrators had trouble accepting criticism. Because they are strong individuals, they think, "I am pretty good at this thing." That was something that most of us had to work on, including myself. I thought it worked really well. I couldn't follow a principal around to really see what to do because they are not going to react naturally. They act naturally with a teacher, and a teacher develops some feelings about all these things. So I thought it was a good evaluation.

Racial Balance and Resegregation

In the paper this week, I see that Princeton is talking about building new schools, and Lincoln Heights is one of the schools they are talking about replacing. But the article said they would still maintain schools in the community. We've always felt that it would be better for Princeton to have maybe four elementary schools, which the whole district would feed into, so you could get a racial balance.

I don't know exactly how it is now, but you used to be able to go to another school in the district if you wanted. Lincoln Heights' kids could choose other schools to go to as long as there was room and as long as it would help the racial balance. But no Black kid outside of Lincoln Heights could go to Lincoln Heights because it would not help the racial balance. But if there were four schools, then you could sort of divide up the numbers a lot better. Anyway, I think a little more thought should go into this whole thing of building new schools because if you want an integrated school district, then you have to somehow balance the groups. Even if the building is built in Lincoln Heights, then you have to get to the point where White kids are coming into Lincoln Heights as well as Black kids going somewhere else. If you just replace schools in the same neighborhood, you are going to always have the same problem.

When the merger first occurred, you had no Blacks living in Sharonville, you had very few Blacks living in Springdale, and very few living in Evandale. But after the merger, people started building houses and now there are a few Blacks in all the neighborhoods. But Lincoln Heights is predominately Black and so is Woodlawn. Because Woodlawn doesn't have as many people and students as Lincoln Heights, Woodlawn kids could go to Lincoln Heights for the first three grades. They would then go to RELIS, the intermediate school on the north side of the district, for fourth, fifth and sixth grades. Schools in the district could send kids to RELIS, based on space availability, and Woodlawn has always sent all of their kids there. A couple of years before I retired we started to open up to the point that if a student wanted to go to another building and if it helped the racial balance of that building, then they could go. So a Woodlawn kid could go to almost any building in the district except Lincoln Heights and maybe Glendale. Glendale was around fifty-fifty at one time, and so we had to be very careful to maintain the balance there.

Well, Glendale got people from Hollydale in there, and they pulled in people from Woodlawn. And they had people who were electing to go to Glendale. This is what happened. The first year after the new superintendent took over, we had to control the numbers that would leave a place like Glendale. Because if you let them do what they wanted to, many of the White kids would be at RELIS, and that is what happened one year. And the parents looked up and their kids were sitting in a predominately Black class. They said, "Wait a minute; this is not how this is supposed to be. How did this happen?" The answer was "Because your neighbor is sending their kids up the street." I think the superintendent had to pull some kids out of that situation because people were mad. They just about destroyed that building for a while. And the Black parents who wanted to have their kids in a more integrated situation—there they were all segregated again. So even the Black parents were concerned about what was going on. You have to be careful in maintaining balance. So if you're going to make these kind of changes, I would think your plan should be "Where do we place these buildings which would make it easy for us there to mix our district?"

No, we did not have an integrated school with segregated classrooms,[43] but we had to work on that pretty heavy to make sure that that didn't happen. It happened more than it should have because we had teachers who could move kids around. Sometimes we'd look up and realize that was what they were trying to do. For instance, RELIS was supposed to be the school for more academically talented kids. Well, if you went by test scores alone, then many of the Black kids who went there wouldn't be able to attend. So you had to look at things other than just the score, for example the work habits of the kid and a lot of other things. Denoyer, the superintendent, had to fight this all the time because there were some parents who wanted to make RELIS a purely academic school that would even throw out some of the White kids that were there. So you had to be sure that did not happen. We wanted to get a good mix of kids, and we found that the kids benefited from that and they did okay. We didn't have students who were so far out of step with the rest of their class. But we had to be very, very careful because we found that a lot of parents only wanted the academically talented kids in their kid's classroom. If you drain all those kids off, you also do something to the rest of your student mix. You take some of that energy away from other classes so you have to be very careful. Some administrators don't have enough guts to make those calls and so they allow the parents to push them into a situation that's not really that good for kids.

Our big problem was the isolation of Lincoln Heights. There were a lot of Black parents who didn't want their kids to go to RELIS for the move into the fourth grade. They wanted their kids to stay close by.[44] And you had to sell them on going to RELIS and taking on RELIS's programs. At one time, RELIS used more of a team-oriented approach where each teacher taught fourth, fifth, and sixth graders. That was the original concept. Then people wanted to make it more of an elitist school and fought against doing that. I don't know where he stands on the issue now, but I think that when the new superintendent came, he moved in that direction. That is what drew so many people out of Glendale. Their kids flocked into RELIS, and they looked up and they had a building in Glendale that they had turned predominately Black over the summer.

This valley was a good place to grow up though. I think it's still a good place to raise your kids. You don't really get the hardcore problems. It used to be better than it is because when you had the valley industries, it was so easy to walk to your jobs. But the way things changed, that makes it a little more difficult. Plus now you have to have more skills. When I worked at Carey's they had very few automated things. You had to pull or push or pick up with your back. And now people need more training and that is really hurting because we have so many people who are just not taking advantage of the situation. But we have a lot of people who are. I go to a golf tournament in Phoenix every year that raises money for minority golfers no matter where they go to school. I run into so many nice people, and there are an awful lot of young adults out there who are doctors, lawyers, and professors. They're doing a lot of things, and we are getting a bigger and bigger group all the time. But we still have so many who are influenced by their environment growing up that they still don't see things. I talk with young people about being successful. I tell them that no matter what color you are, there are certain basic things that you are going to have to do to be successful.

Ernest Ector
Principal, Lincoln Heights Elementary School, 1964–1986

Educational Background

I was born on Jackson Street, on the lower end of Jackson Street—1450 Jackson Street.[45] I went to Grant Street School as a youngster for the first three grades. It was a one-room school on the corner of Grant and Jackson, which had one teacher, Mrs. Shaffer. After those three years I went to Wayne School in Lockland. I wasn't able to go South Woodlawn because we lived below the district line that had been drawn. There was a line a little more than half way up the hill of Jackson Street, and everyone who lived below it had to go to Wayne or some other school. They couldn't go to South Woodlawn. So I went to the Wayne School from the fourth grade through the twelfth, graduating in 1947. After graduating from there I went to Knoxville College one year. I stayed there one year and didn't like the environment, so I transferred to Central State where I graduated in '51. My major was biology and education.

From Teacher to Principal

After graduating from Central State, I came back home and worked at Drake Hospital and a few other places. I didn't like what was going on so I decided I was going into the army. I went into the army in the latter part of '51 and I stayed there until 1955. When I came back home I got more jobs. I worked at the U.S. Health Department and also the post office. While working at the post office, I enrolled in Xavier University and got my masters in counseling in 1957. I began teaching at Lincoln Heights School that year. I wouldn't say I started out to be a teacher. I had thought about going into medicine, but I found that the road was so complex and difficult for me that I went into education. I taught seventh and eighth grade science for two to four years. Then they needed a biology teacher in the high school, and I went over to the high school and taught biology.

Then they wanted someone to work in counseling, and I did a little of that. In the meantime, another position opened up, and I was asked by members of the board to go back to school to get my certification so that I could go into administration. I had to take about three or four courses to get my certificate in administration. I became principal at the elementary school from 1964 to 1986, when I retired. There was a time before the merger[46] when the junior high kids were in my building, and the high school was next door. I was supervising both junior high and elementary students, which caused quite a bit of confusion and was quite difficult to administer. At that time there were about 800 or 900 kids in that building. After the merger in 1970, I remained as principal at the Lincoln Heights facility.

Teaching before the Merger

One of the things that I was doing while I was a teacher was going around getting resources from other places. One of my good friends was Dr. Welling, the optometrist over in East Lockland. He had taken care of me since I was about seven years old when I got my glasses. I would go over there, and he would have these little models and you could see the parts of the eyes and things like that. I would go to the medical doctors and get vertebra. I'd go and beg for those models and I'd use them in class. Some kids and I went over in the creek and got some snakes. Of course, there were a bunch of kids bringing the garter snakes back in their pockets, and we'd have to have a good discussion about not doing that. I'd go out and try to get some things that weren't readily available and try to utilize that to help instruct the kids.

We used to make our own motors. We'd get some copper wire and we'd make our own electric motor. We used to do all kinds of things that the kids enjoyed. I've seen some of them since. They used to come and talk to me about some of the things we used to do. We would try to utilize whatever resources were available because we just didn't have the money to go out and buy things the way we would have liked.

The Merger

The merger did not cause too much apprehension from the elementary students, but there were some concerns. Some kids were concerned about going up there to other Princeton schools. But we weren't too sensitive to the merger because we had the lower grades. The six graders might have had a little bit of concern because they would have to go up to the junior high school.[47]

I don't recall the teachers having too much concern because I think most of them felt that the merger was for the better. Because our salaries were so low, we knew that if we merged with Princeton there would be an improvement. I didn't see a concern about losing jobs because of the merger.[48] If they had concerns like that, I guess it was relieved through the meetings that we had with people from Princeton, particularly Dr. Lucas, who spent a lot of time talking to the teachers about the advantages of merging. One of the problems we had was that we couldn't keep teachers because our salaries were so low. They would come and use us like an internship, and then they would go to Cincinnati.[49] I can't say the elementary was impacted greater than the high school, but I do feel that both the elementary and the high school were affected by the people who chose to go to Cincinnati rather than stay at Lincoln Heights.[50] We just couldn't keep teachers over two or three years, and we had some good teachers, too—people who, we thought, did a good job, but just couldn't give them the salary that they desired.

I believed that the merger would be better academically for the students. I definitely felt that way from the beginning, recognizing that the curriculum at Princeton was so much larger, there were so many other courses there that our little high school could not provide. So yes, we felt that it was a good thing. All the members of the Lincoln Heights school board didn't feel that way though. I know one particular member who was definitely against it, and for years afterward he was going around saying that we shouldn't have merged with Princeton. Basically from what I could gather it was more of that Black pride thing which says "We can provide for our children." We couldn't provide those kids with what they would get up there at Princeton, but he just couldn't see it. For example, the boys had to come from the high school over to the elementary school to take shop, and the girls were coming over to the elementary school to take home economics. That kind of movement alone around the younger children just wasn't beneficial. As far as I know the parents were pretty positive, and I can't recall any negative comments coming from the community. There were some negative comments, I think, coming from Princeton, naturally, but nothing from Lincoln Heights proper.

There were some meetings held prior to the merger when we were going around to different White peoples' houses, and White people were coming down and we were meeting with them at the school. We were in different groups. These were groups set up so that we could try to get to know people in order to make the merger go smoothly. That's when Sam Mays and I were in meetings together. I guess Mr. Holloway was together with someone else. Anyway, Sam and I went to one house of a lady up on Fields Ertel Road—a beautiful home. We just sat down and talked about the merger. I don't recall that lady's name but she was very nice. She was in several meetings with us. In addition, there were meetings at hotels and different places like that as well as at school.

I think another thing that happened that helped to make this community more positive was the fact that when our kids went up there, they were integrated into the flow of things. I had one daughter, JoAnn. She had graduated from Lincoln Heights High School prior to the merger. But Holloway's son, Winny, was the quarterback at Princeton, and they had never had a Black quarterback there before. We had two or three boys who went into basketball and they did well. Then of course, John Hillard, who had been our coach down here, became the basketball coach up there. So there were numerous things that occurred that made it more positive. And every time there was a levy that came forth, Lincoln Heights was one of the communities they could depend upon to be positive and there we were the poorest. We passed the levies all the time. That wasn't true in Sharonville or in Evandale. That's where they'd get the opposition, but Lincoln Heights was always positive.

Immediately after the merger things seemed to change. We began to have meetings with all the administrators from Princeton School District. I remember when we used to get together and have sensitivity training sessions when they wanted to learn more about Blacks. Of course, that offered us an opportunity to get to know and understand some of the feelings of those administrators who were receiving us. One of them particularly, an administrator at a Springdale school, just could not understand and did not like Blacks. He just didn't but he finally came around. He was an old hillbilly from down in Kentucky, and, boy, we had a rough time. But I got to know him; he got to know me. One summer he called me and said "Hey, I want to get some wood and it's down at…" I've forgotten what company it was, but he wanted to go get some lumber from some company down in the West End.[51] He called me and said, "Could you go with me?" I said, "Yes, I will go with you, but why do you want me to go with you?" He said, "I'm just scared." We got to know each other so well that he would tell me that he was just afraid to do things with Black people. He was scared to come to Lincoln Heights, but as time went on, we fell more in line. Not too long ago, he told me to call him; he wanted to go out to lunch with me. So, there were some people who were really sensitive, and they were really concerned but they came right into line after a while. I didn't feel any partiality early on from the other principals. I felt that one principal was not partial, but I learned from others that he was one who was involved in the Evandale incident.[52] He would occasionally make a crack about Lincoln Heights, but he was not one who was afraid to come over like the other guy from Springdale.

Princeton teachers didn't come to teach at Lincoln Heights to any extent until Helen Jones went into personnel at Princeton. She was a principal, and she progressed to personnel around 1974 or '75, somewhere in that time period. There was a ruling that came from the government regarding the fact that the teacher ratio must be representative of the makeup of the entire community. Well, one-third of Princeton was Black, and so that's when they put Helen in to try to straighten things out. So Helen transferred a lot of my teachers. I fought them, because they took some good people, but it didn't do any good. They took the best and put them in the White schools, then she sent us some White teachers. So my staff, which had been all Black suddenly was only one-third Black after two or three years. They wouldn't send White students, just the teachers.[53]

When they opened the Robert E. Lucas Intermediate School (RELIS), that's when they began to get some students from all over the district from the intermediate grades to go there. And that's when some of our kids began to go also. RELIS is in the north end of Sharonville right at the border—the county line. Before the merger Lincoln Heights maintained kindergarten through eighth grades, but after the merger it was a kindergarten through sixth grade school. RELIS had fourth, fifth, and sixth grades. Many of the parents had chosen to send their youngsters to the Robert E. Lucas Intermediate School, but some chose to stay back. After a while, some of the kids that were up there didn't like it, and they wanted to come back. That kind of thing happens.

After the merger, we were able to get better materials. We were involved in the selection of curriculum, books, textbooks, and that kind of thing. We were able to get all kinds of equipment including science equipment. We got everything that the other people had, so that worked out well for us.

My job wasn't easier.[54] I had more things to keep up with and I had more staff members too. I was trying to maintain a staff that was stable, a staff that I could depend on, a staff that was reliable, people that could work together peacefully. That became my greater concern. After that merger and some time had gone by, I think I had one Black teacher, Mrs. Rhodes in the sixth grade, and I think I had one on the fourth grade. I had three teachers on each level—fourth, fifth and sixth—and I ended up with about one Black teacher on each one of those levels. These lower grades had more integration of the White teachers into the classroom, so I ended up with one or two good Black teachers. I tried to keep them around to make the grade level work more coherently. I was also permitted, through Princeton and Helen Jones, to go and recruit. I began to recruit some White teachers I found at Miami University and brought them down. So, there were definitely some advantages that I hadn't had before, and I was pleased with that.

Some of the people, however, who were transferred in from other schools were poor teachers, and I didn't like that. Because it then becomes a difficult task of trying to get rid of them, and that can be really hazardous or hectic. That is what happened when they started integrating staffs. There were some teachers in the other schools that the principals apparently didn't want, so I ended up with some of those characters. And naturally, I didn't want to send them my best, but I didn't have a choice because all my staff was Black. Later I was involved in the interview process because that was one thing that Helen Jones set up. Prior to that time, we had very little input. But Helen believed in the principals interviewing as well as she. We then would get together and talk about whether or not we wanted that individual. At the time I had a staff of approximately 35 to 40 teachers. It is really rough when you have to allow some of them to go, so you try to keep what you can. You have to fight with the personnel people up at central office. I would say, "You can't take that one; you can't take this person." Helen and I used to go round and round, but I lost most of the time because she was the power that be. Florence Snell was one of my main teachers. I had to fight to keep her. She stayed with me the entire time.

Notes

1. This interview with Willis Holloway took place March 14, 2001, at his residence in Lincoln Heights, Ohio.

2. Holloway is referring to the Cincinnati Public School District (CPS) and references the CPS in this manner throughout the interview. The school in Lincoln Heights was not a part of CPS but was initially part of the county system.

3. Lyle was a well-known resident of Lincoln Heights. Most were aware that he owned property on all four corners of Jackson and Leggett streets. My grandparents rented the two-story house on one corner of that intersection for many years and frequented his store across the street. Lincoln Heights School Board Minutes of February 7, 1951, show Lyle in attendance, along with Shands, Hunter, Harvey and Watts, which verifies that he was a member of the Lincoln Heights' board after Lincoln Heights was no longer a part of the Woodlawn School District.

4. Here Holloway is reacting to a question I interjected to clarify the issue concerning Woodlawn's request to the county board of education to redraw their district lines (P. R. Leigh, "Segregation by Gerrymander: The Creation of the Lincoln Heights [Ohio] School District," *Journal of Negro Education* 66, no. 2 [1997]: 121–136). Leigh's documentation does not reveal the political manipulations and negotiations that Holloway reveals in this portion of the interview. Here he states that Lyle was a member of the Woodlawn Board of Education, representing the segregated South Woodlawn School. According to Holloway, some of the White board members convinced Lyle and others to sever themselves from Woodlawn and gain control of their own district.

5. For details on Lincoln Heights' struggle for incorporation, see H. L. Taylor, *The Building of a Black Industrial Suburb: The Lincoln Heights, Ohio Story* (Ph.D. diss., University of New York, Buffalo 1979).

6. In advance of this interview, I had given Holloway preliminary questions. At this point Holloway was likely responding to the following inquiries:

   In Myron Luke's account of the history of the Princeton School District, he reports, "In 1949, the county board of education employed Mr. St. Clair, field agent of the Ohio Department of Education, to make a study of all the local districts in Hamilton County and submit a plan for redistricting. This study recommended that seven districts…be combined….*Lincoln Heights asked to be excluded*" [emphasis added]. Luke does not elaborate further on Lincoln Heights' exclusion from the original Princeton consolidation. To your knowledge did Lincoln Heights ask to be excluded? If so which individual or group from Lincoln Heights made that request? What events or factors led to or contributed to that decision? (See M. Luke, "Twenty-five Years of Progress at Princeton," *Princeton Piper* 17, no. 2, [1981]: 5.)

   I also discuss this exclusion in chapter 4 of this book.

7. In this section, Holloway uses the term "merger" when speaking of the original 1953/5 consolidation of eight county districts to form the Princeton School District. Later in the interview, "merger" is used to discuss Lincoln Heights School District's 1970 annexation to the Princeton School District.

8. I grew up in Lincoln Heights so Holloway is alluding to my awareness of or experience with the racial tensions that were present among the communities. Incidentally, although I attended Lincoln Heights Public Schools for kindergarten through second grades, it was prior to Dr. Holloway's tenure as teacher or administrator in the district.

9. Here Holloway indicates that Sharonville went from county to city status to avoid the inclusion of Lincoln Heights in the original consolidation plan that created the Princeton School District. However Luke reports that the PSD consolidation plan was presented to the county board, and the board passed a resolution that created the district in 1953. Due to court-imposed delays, the Princeton Board of Education was appointed (see M. Luke, "Twenty-five Years of Progress at Princeton"). On the other hand, Sharonville became a city, and, consequently, the PSD became a city district in 1962. This was nine years after the original consolidation plan was presented to the county board of education (see M. Luke, "Princeton History: Excitement, Challenge," *Princeton Piper* 18, no. 1, [1981]: 7). Though Holloway's recollections of specific years for these events—the initial formation of PSD and its change to city status—do not correspond with historical documentation, a newspaper account does verify that many suspected that the motive of Sharonville's change to city status and the PSD to a city district was to avoid the merger or annexation of Lincoln Heights. Interestingly, in 1962 Lincoln Heights successfully petitioned to move from the city status it had attained in 1951 back to county status. Concerning PSD's change to city status, the article states, "There were suspicions that the move also was made to prevent the two adjacent districts—Lincoln Heights and Princeton—from being under the county board at the same time and thus, more easily merged" (from "City Problems of Lincoln Heights Lead to Similar Woes for Schools" *The Cincinnati Enquirer,* 17 June 1970). Holloway's statements that follow this note are in response to the my question about the timeline.

10. Again, even though Holloway's timeline does not coincide with other documentation his arguments are still valid. Lincoln Heights was a city school district until Ohio legislation was passed in 1961 that would allow it to return to the county system. On the other hand Princeton was in the county system until 1962 when Sharonville became a city. If Princeton indeed wanted to avoid the merger or annexation of Lincoln Heights at this point in time, then Holloway's arguments would stand.

11. The rationale offered by Luke in "Princeton History: Excitement, Challenge" for Princeton's change to city status was as follows: "This action was not mandatory, but was enacted at the discretion of the Board, giving Princeton more autonomy and saving about $20,000 annually in contributions to the Hamilton County Board of Education." (p. 7)

12. Holloway is again responding to the report by Luke that stated that Lincoln Heights asked to be excluded from the original consolidation or merger of 1953/5. (See note 5) He is also reacting to a magazine article of 1970 where he was quoted concerning Lincoln Heights' exclusion. The following excerpt was also sent to Holloway as a part of the preliminary interview questions. In an article in *Ohio Magazine* (March 1996), author Lonnie Wheeler reports, "Holloway…was mindful of the fact that *Lincoln Heights had been studiously excluded* from Princeton's (PSD) original consolidation and accepted this as an indication Princeton was not a district in breathless pursuit of integration" [emphasis added].

13. Holloway was adamant about this point. Lincoln Heights could not ask to be excluded from a merger it was unaware of. Though, according to Holloway, Lyle was manipulated into removing Lincoln Heights from the consolidation/merger equation by going along with the Woodlawn board's proposal to remove Lincoln Heights from its district, the Lincoln Heights community was unaware of the Princeton merger in the making. The merger was indeed in the making as evidenced by the 1949 study that recommended to the county board a plan for redistricting by combining seven of the county districts in the valley. The only difference in the 1949 recommendation and the 1953 plan that was approved by the county board was the inclusion of an eighth district, Woodlawn (see Luke, "Twenty-five Years of Progress at Princeton"). Between 1949 and 1953 several things happened that seem to support Holloway's point. In 1950 Woodlawn had its district lines redrawn, and the Lincoln Heights School District was created. After the 1950 census, Lincoln Heights became a city, and its school district moved under city jurisdiction and was no longer the concern of the county. (See G. I. Harris and R. B. Erickson, *A Study of Consolidation and Redistricting in Hamilton County Schools* [Cincinnati: Hamilton County Research Foundation, 1951]: 11; Miami University, Bureau of Educational Field Services, *Lincoln Heights: Its People, Its Schools, Its Future* [Oxford, OH: Author, 1961]: 11–12; Leigh, "Segregation by Gerrymander," 131–133.)

14. Holloway is responding to my comment that Lincoln Heights was incorporated a few years earlier than Evandale so it was already cut out of the General Electric property, though there was still hope in the Lincoln Heights community that they could annex the valuable property. The statements that follow indicate his belief that the incorporation of Lincoln Heights without the valuable property (1946), the incorporation of Evandale with the valuable property (1950), the withdrawal of Lincoln Heights from the Woodlawn School District (1950), and the consolidation plan for the new Princeton district (1949–55) were all connected, and the talks and decisions concerning these events and issues took place simultaneously and heavily influenced each other. (See note 10 and for reference to Evandale's incorporation see G. J. Giglierano and D. A. Overmyer, *The Bicentennial Guide to Greater Cincinnati: A Portrait of Two Hundred Years* [Cincinnati: The Cincinnati Historical Society, 1988]: 577.)

15. In this context, Holloway uses the term "merger" to mean the unification of the various Black subdivisions in the Mill Creek Valley that became the incorporated village and later city of Lincoln Heights.

16. For a map of Lincoln Heights' boundaries, see "Lincoln heights: Now a Chance to Overcome Most Difficulties of the Past," *The Cincinnati Enquirer*, 16 September 1974 (Figure 3 in chapter 3 of this book). This map also shows lines indicating the industrial land that was eliminated when Lincoln Heights was incorporated.

17. This irregular boundary is difficult to depict on a map. Holloway is referring to the fact that Lockland was allowed to incorporate land on the west side of Wayne Avenue. This land included industrial property which ended at or near the Lincoln Heights residence of Guy Westmoreland. However land on the east side of that same strip of Wayne Avenue belonged to the village/city of Lincoln Heights but contained mostly residences and a few small businesses.

18. One law that Holloway is speaking of concerns the fact that the state of Ohio would no longer pay the tuition for students to attend schools outside their district. Since initially Lincoln Heights did not have a high school within its boundaries, students attended neighboring schools as indicated earlier in the interview. Holloway contends that the state discontinued the practice of paying this tuition by enacting a law. The second component of this law, or the second distinct law, actually prohibited students from attending schools in other districts. Holloway indicated that these laws were enacted circa 1956 just prior to the building and opening of the new Lincoln Heights High School.

19. Here Holloway is responding to my comment that only two of the eight districts that would eventually merge into the Princeton School District had high schools within their boundaries. Therefore, Princeton's merger of 1955 was just ahead of the law that required students to attend schools in their district, a law that in Holloway's recollection was passed in 1956.

20. In the pre-interview questions I asked Holloway to respond to the following:
Before Lincoln Heights became a part of the Princeton School District, the latter provided the former with economic resources to build a new high school. Myron Luke reports, "In December of 1957 Princeton transferred to Lincoln Heights $6,500,000 of tax valuation of the General Electric Company plant in Evandale. This doubled the tax valuation of that district and enabled them to build a new high school."

In a 1970 newspaper article in *The Cincinnati Enquirer*, "Lucas recalled that in 1956–57, *at the request of Lincoln Heights*, Princeton transferred a $6.5 million General Electric building to Lincoln Heights. 'A year or two later, however, GE leased the building to someone else and the value went down,' Lucas said. *But the transfer was 'what they (Lincoln Heights officials) wanted at the time. They did not want to merge'*" (from "City Problems of Lincoln Heights Lead to Similar Woes for Schools" *The Cincinnati Enquirer*, 17 June 1970) [emphasis added].

21. I asked Holloway if Lucas had been directing the creation of the Princeton District before his official appointment and asked how Lucas came to be named superintendent.

22. I asked if Holloway had much contact with Lucas after Holloway became superintendent of Lincoln Heights School District in 1960.

23. Here Holloway is talking about challenges that emerged from the early to the late 1960s that caused him to move toward a merger.

24. I had asked Holloway if he were totally stressed out during this time period.

25. I had asked Holloway if the first meeting with the superintendents of the districts mentioned above came before Lincoln Heights' school charter had been revoked.

26. The local superintendents involved were Princeton, Lockland, Wyoming, and, of course, Lincoln Heights. These were the districts contiguous with Lincoln Heights.

27. I was surprised by the statement that Wyoming claimed to be a poor school district in light of the fact that I knew the community to be quite wealthy. Holloway explains that they were poor only in terms of how much money they receive from industrial taxes.

28. In a list of pre-interview questions, I asked Holloway how Princeton had secured that tax duplicate in the merger negotiations.

29. I had asked Holloway if there was ever any talk of giving or transferring money to Lincoln Heights to put it in a better economic situation or was that something that he and the rest of the citizens that went to the Feds did not want at that time.

30. This interview with Eddie Starr took place March 13, 2001, at his residence in Woodlawn, Ohio.

31. St. Simon's Elementary School was a parochial school within the boundaries of Lincoln Heights. This school had an all-Black student body and was run by Episcopalian nuns.

32. I attended St. Simon's during Dr. Starr's tenure there and he was my eighth grade teacher.

33. Starr is responding to my question, "What drew you to Lincoln Heights High School?"

34. I had asked Starr about the pressures that caused Cincinnati Public Schools to begin hiring Black teachers at the secondary level.

35. Here Starr is discussing the same problem that Holloway outlined. Lincoln Heights would bring in new teachers who would gain a couple of years of experience only to leave to work in Cincinnati Public Schools for a higher salary.

36. Starr is responding after I asked whether he had opportunities after the merger to meet with Black students to keep them on track and give them advice or had most of his opportunities come after he found out there was going to be a merger.

37. Starr is characterizing the thinking and concerns of some Black families who were already in the Princeton district. He is responding to my comment concerning the fact that before the merger some Lincoln Heights families had moved in order to become a part of the Princeton District. I was questioning whether these particular Black families objected to more Black families being included in the district.

38. Here Starr uses "merger" to refer to the 1970 merger or annexation of the recently defunct Lincoln Heights School District with the Princeton School District.

39. Starr is responding to my comments. I noted that it was interesting that he talked about his role in coordinating the programs because there was no mention of this coordination in Lucas's report (see Lucas, 1976). I pointed out that the Lucas report did say that many of the people in the community, both Black and White parents in Princeton district, were afraid that the transfer would destroy the Princeton schools. They were concerned for the safety of their children and concerned that the academic standards of the school would be lowered. But in talking about these phases he seemed to indicate that the eighth grade children went directly to Princeton and the others stayed behind because of a lack of space. Starr's first response to these comments was "That was a nice way for them to say it but wasn't true." He then went on to explain the role that space played in the merger.

40. The "original merger" that Starr refers to here is the 1950s consolidation of the eight school districts into the Princeton School District.

41. In speaking of the overlap, Starr was responding to my further comments about the Lucas report that stated "Due to the crowded situation the Princeton High School will operate a two-period overlap..." I had commented, "Okay, it does say that all the students in the seventh, eighth, and ninth grades of the two districts would be put together immediately, this was the first year, and that Lincoln Heights High School, tenth, eleventh, twelfth, would become part of the Princeton High School even though space was not available in the main campus to bring all of them to that facility the first year. In other words, most of

their classes would be held in the former Lincoln Heights High School, but they would have an integrated Princeton High School staff. Then they talk about the ability to take courses. But there was no mention of this fear of them not being able to handle the curriculum."

42. Robert E. Lucas Intermediate School (RELIS) is an intermediate school in the Princeton School District.

43. I asked Starr if the Princeton district ran schools that were integrated in theory but had segregated classrooms in reality. I asked if academic tracking had contributed to segregating Black students together in certain classes.

44. Even after the merger, the Princeton district maintained the old Lincoln Heights Elementary School in the Lincoln Heights community, which included kindergarten through sixth grade.

45. This interview with Ernest Ector took place March 15, 2001, at his residence in Lincoln Heights, Ohio.

46. In this interview, Ector uses "merger" to refer to the merger or annexation of Lincoln Heights School District with the Princeton School District.

47. After the merger the seventh, eighth, and ninth grade students went to the junior high schools outside of Lincoln Heights.

48. Here Ector is responding to my question concerning whether the Lincoln Heights teachers were concerned about losing their jobs as a result of the merger.

49. Ector is referring to teachers leaving the Lincoln Heights schools to teach in the Cincinnati public schools.

50. I had asked if Ector thought that the elementary school was more or less affected by the lack of resources and the inability to retain teachers than the high school.

51. The West End is a predominately Black area in downtown Cincinnati. For a history of the development of this Black ghetto along the Ohio river basin, see Taylor (1993).

52. Ector is making reference to Evandale's acquisition of the General Electric Plant during its incorporation procedures. See chapter 3, "Setting the Stage."

53. I had asked Ector if he had gotten any White students at the Lincoln Heights facility after the merger. His answer was "No. No. No. No. No. They wouldn't…didn't do that. They wouldn't do that, no. I know there would have been a fight then. No, just the teachers."

54. Since he had more resources after the merger, I had asked Ector if his job was easier.

CHAPTER 8

The Teachers

A three-hour interview with Florence Snell provided windows into Lincoln Heights Elementary School classrooms preceding, during, and after the merger of PSD and LHSD. Mrs. Snell began a career in public school education in the late 1950s, teaching third grade for eight years and kindergarten for thirteen years. She remained in the Lincoln Heights Elementary School building after the merger until her retirement.

Flora Alexander shared her life and work in Lincoln Heights in a ninety-minute interview. Mrs. Alexander began her teaching career in a parochial school with a Black student body in the community of Lincoln Heights. In the early 1960s, she accepted the position of dean of girls in the public Lincoln Heights School District. Mrs. Alexander provided enrichment programs and counseled high school girls until the merger of PSD and LHSD. In the new Princeton School District, Mrs. Alexander worked as counselor for junior high school boys and girls until her retirement.

Florence Snell
Teacher Lincoln Heights Elementary School, 1960–1981

Educational Background

I was born in Elmwood Place on May 18, 1921.[1] When my husband asked me if I would be willing to move to Lincoln Heights, he seemed concerned that I might object to living there because of the rumors of the school district. I immediately said yes, even though most of my classmates and friends from Hartwell High had told me why they were at Hartwell and not at Lincoln Heights. My immediate response was yes even though I knew the situation that existed. My daughter Jinada was five years old at that time, and she was attending kindergarten at Wyoming, and my daughter Lynn was eight weeks old. When we moved here in September, I still was in need of a home for my children, so I immediately said yes. But really we've resided here forty-four years, and I wouldn't move any place else if I had the opportunity. We've had our ups and downs, but this is where my friends were and my schoolmates were.[2]

Of course in Elmwood we did not have a high school, so we had a choice of going to five different schools. I chose Hartwell because it was closest to Elmwood. At that time there were prejudices and integration at the other schools near by. St. Bernard was also close by, but there were no Blacks going to St. Bernard schools. I chose Hartwell because both Hartwell and St. Bernard were close to us and in walking distance. However, Elmwood paid our tuition and gave us car fare tickets.

We moved to Lincoln Heights in 1958. I knew something was going on because some of those students who were at Hartwell attended Wayne.[3] They were renovating Wayne, and those students had to be moved to Hartwell, the next closest high school, until the renovation was complete. Students who had been at Hartwell two years were allowed to stay, but those who were just freshmen and sophomores had to return to Wayne. These were students from Lincoln Heights and Lockland.

From Hartwell I went to Wilberforce University.[4] I was totally embarrassed there because of my lack of knowledge of my own people, as I had never gone to a Black school. Naturally the students made fun of me or any others that were in the same situation, because we didn't know about people like Frederick Douglass. We didn't know about the Black newspapers like the *Pittsburgh Courier*. When I went to Black history classes, I just felt terrible. I admired my teachers. In fact, most of my writings home were about my teachers. I was surprised that I had a Black teacher. That really meant something, and they were very hard on us, too.

I majored in home economics and had planned on teaching in that area. But at that time, there were only two home economics teachers in a high school and two industrial arts teachers. Consequently, after I'd finished school, it was hard to get a job in my field. I graduated in 1945, and I worked in the city one year with handicapped people and taught them how to sew and embroider on nylon and other new materials. After that I worked at Santa Maria Institute, a day care center, for five years, and during that time, Jinada was born. They called me back when I was pregnant with Lynn but I didn't go back.

At Santa Maria I was the only one eligible for head teacher there because they already had people there with only high school educations. They had to put me in that position because Montessori came in, and we were required to take courses. I was the only one eligible to take the course, so they put me in as head teacher. I took the Montessori courses from a certified Montessori teacher from Italy. I don't recall her name, but I do know she was the teacher at the University of Cincinnati where the course was offered. Of course, in home economics, there were so many things you could go into, but I was eligible for the job at Santa Maria and they couldn't pass that up. I didn't have a problem with that because I enjoyed working with children, and it just added to my experience. That experience helped later when I applied for an elementary certificate. I went back to the diocese to get credit for those years I spent there.

I was the only Black teacher at Santa Maria, and there were few Black children in the area. It was located at Thirteenth and Republic streets, where there are many Blacks now. When I was there, mountain people were coming from Kentucky, and our purpose, of course, was to encourage the parents not to keep the older children home because there was a decent place for children to be. And yet the women wanted the same things that they found other women having, although their husbands did not want them to work. They were able to work by keeping their older kids home to take care of the other children. We went from home to home telling them what they were eligible for, a decent place for their children to be. It was interesting and I was treated royally.

Teaching in Lincoln Heights

I never tried to advance myself at Santa Maria, but they advanced me just because of my eligibility. They wanted me to come back, but at that time I had two children; I didn't want that. I had a small day care center here which you were part of.[5] There were several other influential people who suggested that I apply at the Lincoln Heights school. I wasn't that interested in applying for a job at Lincoln Heights until I was told that home economics was available. I let them know that I was interested.

Jinada had attended St. Simon's but was at Lincoln Heights at the time. When that job was offered, she begged me not to take home economics. "Mom, we don't have materials; our sewing machines are all messed up; they had to cut the gas off on our stoves. Miss Barnett is having a problem." All Jinada had asked me for was a yard of unbleached muslin material, and everything that they did was mostly by hand. I really think Miss Barnett was capable, but due to a lack of materials, there was only so much she could do. That's when I think it first hit me. I wasn't a part of Lincoln Heights' schools, but it was through Jinada complaining that I became aware of the resource problems. Lynn had also attended St. Simon's but would be attending third grade at Lincoln Heights. When I had interest, I didn't want to teach third grade because Lynn was going into the third grade. The reason I mention this is because the job that I was later offered was third grade, and I didn't want her in my class. The one job that was available to me was to be a substitute teacher. This was in September of 1960. Later I was hired as the first permanent substitute and was assigned a third grade class. I was a long-term substitute for about two months, which made me eligible for a regular teaching job the following year.

Substituting was hectic. I really wore my knees out praying, because I had never taught third grade. If they had put me in kindergarten, I think I would have done better. But through prayer and assistance from the older teachers, I did well. However, there was lack of materials. I had six math books and about thirty students. There were about four third grade classes, and this was the top class. I had six books until one of the young Black teachers said, "If you don't tell Mr. Spell, I'm going down and get you some books." My pride wouldn't allow her to do that for me, so I went down and asked him for more books. Mr. Spell was the principal when I was hired. It was then that I found it difficult because of lack of materials in the class and the low salary compared to other schools. The school was rundown, particularly the restrooms; they were in the basement and it was dark and dismal. Classes were overcrowded. I taught third grade eight years and did very well the first year. As I look back there are lawyers, writers, and doctors who came from my class. Later when I taught kindergarten, I had forty-four students.

When I accepted kindergarten with those forty-four children, I was upset that I couldn't get along with them, and I thought maybe it was because of my lack of experience. I didn't know what it was, but there were too many children in one room. I had friends from the city, both are deceased now, and one was a social worker who visited maybe four or five schools. The other was a master teacher, Mrs. Hicks, from Wyoming. I contacted Mrs. Hicks and told her that I was in trouble, I didn't know what was happening, and I didn't know what was going on. I had so many children and no help. My friend, the social worker, told me that Title IV allowed schools to have helpers. At the time she couldn't find the material but she was sure of it. I said, "Before I go to our social worker, I want to be sure that you are right." I went to our social worker at Lincoln Heights who was not aware of Title IV but said he would look it up. He looked it up, and they hired a helper for each class.

There was a time when we were asked to loan the school our salary, which we as teachers agreed to do. We signed contracts, and we were reimbursed monthly when they received the money from the state. There was a lot of turmoil, and I didn't really understand it but they made it clear to us that by signing this contract, we would get our money back and we did. I did not really feel like I had a choice.[6] Because the teachers went along with it, I think they understood it. Maybe it was because the older teachers understood what was going on in the community and in the state, or they accepted it. But my choice was to stay there because I needed to work and I needed a job.

In the meantime, when I first started teaching, I only had a temporary certificate so I had to go to night school and summer school. It took me two years to get my permanent certificate for the elementary grades. I took graduate courses because I was thinking I would get my masters. However, I got a masters equivalent but not a masters degree. The 150 credit hours gave me the same salary as someone with a masters, so they called it a masters equivalent.

I think the parents were concerned about the schools because they more or less had knowledge of segregation. Of course, some were very professional people and felt concerned about some of the things they saw at Lincoln Heights. They also saw things at other schools that weren't available at Lincoln Heights. But the teachers worked hard, and we were only given about $10 per school year for little things we wanted in our classroom. We had to order everything and we were limited to $10 for a whole year until we went into Princeton. What could we buy then? Puzzles maybe. So we made a lot of our materials and supplemented with pictures from magazines and things like that.

And then too, I think that we were taught things to do in our college classrooms. I really believe our college backgrounds, as far as what we were taught, were different than they are now. I also experienced that difference in one of the graduate classes. We were all adults, but half way through the course we felt that if we gave a different answer from what the professor had said, it was wrong. So you seldom saw a hand up; you just listened. I experienced that. "Do what I say do or what the book says do and whatever is old fashioned, forget it." A couple of White people quit that class because they were working like I was and couldn't tolerate that attitude. They were apparently older and more experienced than I was, but I felt it too. But I was seeking my certificate, so I stayed. I wanted to meet the requirements, but it really didn't meet my needs.

Former students, who had become parents, called me back after I retired and asked me what they should do, what teacher I recommended. Or they would see me and say, "Well, you did a lot for me." If I said to them, "I must have been pretty mean for you to remember me." They'd say, "No, I learned something in your room." Those things were rewarding. I have a better feeling now than I had when I was there. Of course, I never felt that I was the best teacher, but I felt that I was more concerned than many others. I brought children home on my lunch hour, gave them a bath, put their clothes in the washer and dryer and took them back. If I were to do that now they would arrest me. But how could I stay in the room with an odor. Once a year, I'd say at the beginning of the year, Mr. Ector, the principal, would always have little panties available for the children who would wet themselves or who came to school with soiled pants.

When I was at Lincoln Heights there were excellent teachers.[7] Maybe half of those teachers are gone now because of age. I compared Lincoln Heights with Wyoming, which is supposed to be the elite and is where my grandchildren go. The teachers in Wyoming were not doing the job that they were doing at Lincoln Heights. I think because my daughters did well and the teachers were older, especially the Black teachers, I never had a problem with them attending Lincoln Heights.

Teaching after the Merger

I was at Lincoln Heights after the merger and I would say that I did get merit pay for five years. They stopped that because of complaints. And of course, the other teachers accused me by saying that all I did was decorate my room. But sometimes I was there until six o'clock whereas they left right after the children left or walked out with them. But I knew that when I got home I had a lot to do, and my interest was at school. I supplemented materials even after we were given more money, maybe $25 per year. Also, after the merger we were given a lot of things that teachers just asked for. They didn't give us the money for these things, but they bought them for us.

My fear going into Princeton was that I would be sent to another school. I think much of that had to do with my age and my fear as a Black teacher. But we were given a buddy, a Princeton teacher, and my buddy was a true

Christian lady. I had a hidden fear that I would be given a position that I was not qualified for. But my White buddy was a Christian person and assured me that I was okay. She was from Sharonville. That scared me to death because she invited me to a candle party in the evening and I got lost and I said, "I don't know. Are they planning to lynch me?" I accepted a position in the summer school in which I conducted a reading activity for preschoolers and kindergarteners. I was able to go to all seven schools that summer. I was relaxed; I felt good; I could go anywhere. But what really relieved me was when Mr. Ector said, "Don't move Snell." That relieved me.

In the end, I was glad the merger occurred. I think, as I look back, it was done smoothly. But just personally, I guess I think overall, I was thinking about all the children. Lynn was more or less given more than Jinada because by the time Lynn entered high school Lincoln Heights' students had been in with Princeton longer. She had more opportunities for scholarships and for taking part in general activities. I think when Lynn went in, they even had a Black choir. They established some things of their own, as they even do now, which they never had before. I really feel that John Hillard, the athletic coach, was a great help and so was Mr. Starr, the high school principal.

After the merger, I still I felt comfortable with my daughters at Lincoln Heights, especially with Jinada because she was over at the high school. The White teachers she had were good; her English teacher, in particular, was excellent. Naturally there were prejudices felt but things went rather smoothly because they had security guards as they got on the bus. The first year, they really weren't equipped for that many children to go to Princeton, so they put them in warehouses. They had classrooms in warehouses so the children were bused. However, the ninth grade stayed at Lincoln Heights. As they finished the transition, eventually the students went to Princeton.

My daughter Lynn was at Princeton, but Jinada's classes were back and forth between Lincoln Heights and the main Princeton school. Their real interest was in the athletes because we had gone to the state championships in basketball. Of course John Hillard and other Black teachers were concerned and able to speak up without a lot of turmoil.

Jinada's class was the first class that graduated during the transition. There was a graduation at Lincoln Heights, which was very tearful. It was outdoors on the lawn, and it was very, very tearful. I mean it was just like they had lost their last friend. Really. It was very touching. At first there were two graduations, but in the end Lincoln Heights went in with Princeton.

But from the parents that I've talked to lately I know that they're blaming the younger teachers for not teaching their children or wanting to teach their children. I disagree with that because when we did integrate, there were White teachers at Lincoln Heights, which fulfilled the requirement of a 40/60 ratio. When we went into the Princeton district, the government required a 40–60 equivalent, that meant forty percent Black to sixty percent White. There were those that wanted to stay, so they stayed there and retired. Those that didn't want to stay left the next year or the next two years. Today, parents are thinking it's the White young teachers—that's who they're putting the blame on. But I believe they aren't taught in the colleges how to teach well. There are always going to be some that are lax, that only care about the money. But there are some dedicated young Black and White teachers. But that was twenty years ago. Things have really changed.

Another thing that has changed is family life. I think, more or less, if a child is trained at home, whether he is at the bottom of the scale or the top of the scale, he has good training at home and good manners at home. Now teachers are having problems, and I'm experiencing some of that at my church in my Sunday School class. The children are different. One parent said to me, just this past Sunday, "Sister, I see that you're harder on the children this year or this generation than you were with us." And I said, "Well, your parents taught you how to behave. I didn't have to have that problem. All I had to do was look at you." But now it's just different, and it is the family whether they're professional people or people who have meager jobs. You usually think that professional people have better manners, but I can't say that is true because parents don't really have the time to take with their children.

Flora Alexander
Dean of Girls, Lincoln Heights High School, 1967–1970
Counselor, Princeton Junior High School, 1970–1998

Educational Background

I'm a Buckeye. I was born in Lockland, Ohio, on Maple Street. I was born, reared, and I walked the streets of Lockland.[8] I was the person that went to the store for everybody in the neighborhood. If they wanted somebody to go to the store, I would go to the store. I grew up and went to Lockland Wayne School.

We've always been segregated. There is a West Lockland and East Lockland. We lived in West Lockland, and East Lockland was where the high school was. My brother went to the White high school when he was a kid. That was a bone of contention for a long while. Everything on the west side was for Black folks, and the east side and Reading was for Whites. In fact we hated Reading—Reading and Norwood; they hated us and we hated them. Parents wouldn't let their children go to Reading or Norwood unless they had a reason to be there, and there was a school activity going on. There were always fights, but my family was never involved.

But we were very segregated; all Black over here and all White over there. In fact, a lady I worked with at Princeton went to East Lockland High, and she recalls a lot of things. When polio became very crippling and kids were catching it, there was no place to swim for the Black kids. We went to Hartwell, right down the street from here on Galbraith Road. We had to walk to Hartwell Recreation Center to swim. There were certain days and hours that we could do that. The same was true for the Carthage Fair in Carthage. Every year they would let us out of school a half day on Friday to go to the county fair. This is how we spent our youth, but those were enjoyable days. Also, the church and the YMCA were focal points for us as kids coming up. Things took place at the Y in Lockland and the school.

All the activities centered around school, and I was very active. I joined organizations and clubs because I knew that was a way of getting involved. I was a cheerleader all four years in high school and all four years in college.

When I finished eighth grade I went to the high school, Lockland Wayne, which had already been built. It was an addition to the elementary school. During the summer they simply built the high school and just attached it on to the elementary school. I graduated from college in 1949 and from high school in 1945. Tomorrow, the 30th of May, was my graduation for my baccalaureate.

After high school I went on to Knoxville College in Knoxville, Tennessee. The city of Knoxville was segregated, very segregated. There was a Colored side and a White side. Knoxville College was all Black. Knoxville was a southern city in the deep South. It was considered very Southern. In fact, it was said that during the Civil War a lot of battles were fought on the campus of Knoxville College. They pointed out certain spots and certain streets where the soldiers fought. The campus was beautiful, I thought. I was able to attend because of the Giovannis. Gus Giovanni—Nikki's daddy, Bill

Lovelace—an attorney, Mr. Reardon, and another attorney were instrumental in getting me a scholarship. I had a four-year scholarship.

My daddy said, "You can't go, girl. We don't have any money to send you to school. You just get a job and work. No, you can't go." I said, "Oh, daddy I'm going to school. If I just stay a semester, I'm going to school." I had no idea what a semester meant. I went. Nikki's parents, Mr. G. and Mrs. G., both finished at Knoxville College, and he said to my daddy, "I can guarantee you that I can get her a scholarship." And I got a scholarship. Then he said, "I can go another step and say that we'll find her a job and you don't have to worry." Daddy said, "But we don't have any money!" And Mr. G. said, "Oh, don't worry about that, Mr. Fletcher, she will work. If she is willing to work, she can work her way through." And I did. I worked my way through college. I had a good job. I worked in the business office, in the registrar's office, ran the student post office, and worked with student accounts. Mr. Giovanni had taught at Lockland Wayne off and on. He also taught at South Woodlawn and Lockland but more part time at Lockland. He also taught me how to play tennis. He was athletically inclined and he was in charge of the boys' activities.

I was the very first in my family to go to college. I was determined because as a kid growing up, all I did was go to church and go to school. I was actively involved in school and I admired all my teachers. All my teachers were beautiful. They would encourage us to go to school and they would tell us about their college days. I always said "I want to be a part of that." I always said, "I'm going to school, I'm going to college." It all started my freshman year, but as a sophomore at high school I knew I was going away to school. I was interested in the sciences, so I took biology as a major and physical education as a minor. I graduated with a B.S.

After I graduated, I got married and went back to Knoxville because the guy I married is from Knoxville. I lived in Knoxville for three years. I worked for a local doctor in Knoxville, not in the school system. When I first came back to Ohio, I wanted to teach, but I worked at Good Sam Hospital as a ward secretary working on birth certificates in the OB ward. That's when they would tell me, "Oh, you're a college graduate; you have too much education to be working here." They were so nice to me. That's the job they gave me. I typed birth certificates and passed out materials to new mothers.

Entering Teaching

But my desire to really teach came after I finished college and was married. My husband and I had jobs at this all-Black school in Mound Bayou, Mississippi. It is a town similar to Lincoln Heights; it was all Black. It was known as the first all-Black city south of the Mason-Dixon line. We had jobs as a pair—a team. I was going to teach the sciences, and he was going to be the coach and teach also. That summer he had to go earlier because in the South you started coaching early even though they had planted cotton, and the kids got out of school to harvest the cotton. He had to go in August. I was so excited and I was just planning to go. He called and said, "You don't want to come down here; you don't want to come down here." I said, "Oh yes, I do; I want to go." He was already there. I said, "I'm coming," so I did. But I stayed one night. During that time you stayed with families.

There were no hotels or anything, and I was afraid of mice and rats. I saw a mouse during breakfast, and I was scared to death. The couple served the best food; it was delicious, and the place was clean, but I didn't want to stay. My husband said, "I tried to tell you." But I felt guilty after leaving there because those kids were so needy compared to us and the things we had. They were so needy. I felt so guilty. So when the job became available at St. Simon's, I decided to teach. I was going to make it a life's vocation because I did not follow through on what I could have done in Mississippi for all those little Black kids.

Mrs. Giovanni was teaching at St. Simon's, and Father Harrison was getting ready to go back to New York. His wife was teaching so they needed a teacher. They told me who to call. I called Sister Whitaker or Sister Virginia, that's how I got the job. I met Sister Althea. I think it was 1951 when I began teaching fifth grade.[9] I loved it. That was home. I had learned about St. Simon's from high school and from learning to play tennis there. Also, because of the association with Lockland Wayne we knew about Lincoln Heights and the school situation.

There was an entirely different kind of student at St. Simon's. There was a religious atmosphere and the routine of going to church. There was the belief in a higher being and that somewhere in your life you are going to have to give an account of all the negative things that you did, that God was watching you. Going to mass and high holy days were very meaningful to a lot of the boys and girls. We followed a course of study but could put almost anything in the curriculum that we wanted as long as it was in the guidelines of the Ohio state department. I never will forget that one science project was to have a garden every spring in the back of the tennis court. The boys would break the ground and plant. We had tomatoes, corn, onions, and things like that. Everybody had a week to care for the garden because it was a class project. When the weather was good and it produced, we would eat the food. It was a little small plot where the tennis courts were.

That is also where we had gym. I taught physical education at St. Simon's. We played kick ball and I pitched for both sides.

There was rivalry between the kids from St. Simon's and the kids from Lincoln Heights' public schools. The Lincoln Heights students resented the students from St. Simon's because they felt that St. Simon's students thought they were better. This was because the average parent at St. Simon's was educated. They had finished high school, and some had some college training. There was a difference in their expectancies for their children, and the socioeconomic standards were entirely different. At that time Lincoln Heights' homes were substandard. They would build the basement, and that is as far as some of them got. As a family made money, they would continue to build their houses; however, there were some families that never got out of the basement.

Counseling at Lincoln Heights

I had always said that Mr. Holloway's kids were so bad that I could not teach down there. I said, "I will never teach at Lincoln Heights." But I did. I taught at Lincoln Heights for three years.

An opportunity opened up when Mr. Holloway got some federal funds to do something for the kids in Lincoln Heights for the summer. He wanted an enrichment program, and he needed somebody to run the program. He asked me if I would be willing, so that summer I started working at Lincoln Heights. I had worked the summer before for Lockland running a recreational program. I would bring sandwiches and something to drink, and I would show movies. It was an enrichment program for kids. The program at Lincoln Heights was so well received that Holloway asked me if I would please stay during the fall, and I did. I went in as dean of girls at Lincoln Heights. I was a counselor because the girls were having babies, and Holloway felt it was because health and hygiene was not being taught. Actually, the guys were giving the girls a hamburger and a bottle of pop and getting in the car and doing what they wanted to do. I brought a total program, not just sex education. There was an awareness of how to dress and how to act.

I was there three years before we merged with Princeton. I did regret leaving St. Simon's, but I was doing beautiful work because you could see a change in the girls. You could see them being concerned. I would tell them, "You don't let boys paw all over you just because they want to." After basketball games, the girls, instead of going home, would stand out in front of the school and hug and kiss. I would say, "No, he needs to respect you. You have to carry yourself so that a guy can respect you." I saw a difference; I saw a change. I talked to the girls individually, and their typing teacher also had a big influence on them. Her last name was Morris, and she belonged to Mt. Zion Church. She was a great influence. She was very ladylike, and they respected her. She did things right and it made a difference.

The Merger

I worked hard during the merger. I was so tired because I was like the liaison person between the coffee clutches. Helen Jones got tired too, and she would send me to talk to the faculty. That is why I know that Whites are afraid of Blacks. I was told that they didn't know how to take Black people. We don't want any more than what's due us. And we don't have to fight for it anymore the way they did in the South and in the Civil War and with Dr. King. We don't have to do that. As Holloway used to say, "You either marry us or we'll take you to court." You take your "druthers." Which would you rather do? Helen was too tired to make it to the meetings with parents in the various communities; they were really afraid. I was meeting with White parents to let them know that "We don't want any more than you want. Black parents want what you want. We want to get along, and we want to see a smooth transition from one setting to the other."

In Lincoln Heights, Holloway would have meetings, and he would do it street by street and name by name and according to grade levels. He tried to get the parents out to make them aware of what was happening and what was going to happen. The churches were for the merger. You could contact Black people through the local churches and the ministerial alliance. During that time Otis Moss was our minister at Mt. Zion, and he was very adamant as far as civil rights were concerned. He and Dr. King were very close. When they started the Southern Christian Leadership organization, our church spearheaded a part of that. Reverend Moss had children old enough to see what was happening. He was born in the South and being a Southerner and a Morehouse man, he knew what had happened to education. He knew that we have not had the advantages that White folks have had because, number one, our textbooks were always outdated whereas they always had the latest edition of everything. He wasn't afraid to stand on his soap box and talk to people and have mass meetings.

Counseling at Princeton

I had become a counselor through the grandfather clause because of the work I had done with the merger. Of course, my experience also warranted that I could become a counselor. I worked with the boys and girls. I did pretty much the same thing only it was a more developed pattern. In addition to sex education we were concerned with the social behavior of boys as well as girls. This was in the junior high school; seventh and eighth grade boys and girls. We developed our own ongoing curriculum, beginning with September when students started and continuing throughout the entire school year. We also developed a health program, and we had groups talk about social situations.

I counseled some of the same families in Princeton that I had counseled in Lincoln Heights. That's why you knew what the problems were going to be. There are family problems that will follow you. It was a constant teaching thing. The anger in some was so deep-seated that you couldn't reach them. But then others, you could talk to them and you could show them right from wrong. One of the biggest things that I found in my counseling, although it would make me so angry, is that everybody wants to be loved—all of us. I want to be loved. That's the biggest thing with young girls is that they will listen to boys with a line of jive that will make them think that they are "God's gift." I was telling my sister the other day that my mother used to always say, "upper persuasion leads to lower invasion." And it wasn't until I became an adult that I understood what she was talking about.

Notes

1.   This interview took place April 19, 2001, at the interviewee's residence in Lincoln Heights, Ohio.

2. Some of Mrs. Snell's closest friends moved to Lincoln Heights after high school and other former classmates and friends had already resided in Lincoln Heights before she moved from Elmwood.

3. Here I had pointed out that she moved to Lincoln Heights the year the new high school was opened. She is implying that she was aware of the situation because her ex-classmates had informed her. She is referring to the students from Lincoln Heights and Lockland who were attending the all-Black Lockland Wayne High School. She met and became friends with these students when they attended Hartwell High School when Wayne was being renovated.

4. Wilberforce University was an historically Black institution in Wilberforce, Ohio.

5. As an adolescent/teenager I worked for Mrs. Snell in her home-based day care center.

6. She was responding to my question as to whether she felt she had a choice in loaning her salary to the school system.

7. I had commented that in a recent newsletter, I had read that Lincoln Heights' children were still falling behind on standardized testing. I asked if that had always been a problem. Her immediate response was, "No, Well, no I really don't go along with that because when I was at Lincoln Heights there were excellent teachers."

8. This interview with took place May 29, 2001, at the interviewee's current residence.

9. I attended St. Simon's Elementary School for grades three through eight, and Mrs. Alexander was my fifth grade teacher.

Bibliography

Aaron, D. (1992). *Cincinnati, queen city of the west: 1819–1838.* Columbus, OH: Ohio State University Press.

Becker, G. S. (1964). *Human capital: A theoretical and empirical analysis, with special reference to education.* New York, NY: Columbia University Press.

Bell, D. A. (1980). *Brown* and the interest-convergence dilemma. In D. Bell (Ed.), *Shade of Brown: New perspectives on school desegregation* (pp. 90–106). New York, NY: Teachers College Press.

———— (1987). *And we are not saved: The elusive quest for racial justice.* New York, NY: BasicBooks.

———— (1992). *Faces at the bottom of the well.* New York, NY: BasicBooks.

———— (1995). Property rights in whiteness: Their legal legacy, their economic costs. In R. Delgado (Ed.), *Critical race theory: The cutting edge.* (pp. 75–83). Philadelphia, PA: Temple University Press.

Bernstein, M. F. (1996). Racial gerrymandering. *The Public Interest, 122,* 59–69.

Borg, W. R., & Gall, M. D. (1989). *Educational research.* New York, NY: Longman.

Bowman, M. J. (1991). Educational inequalities and opportunity in economic perspective. *Oxford Review of Education, 17*(2), 189–209.

Brinkman v. Gilligan, Civil Action No. 72–137 (1973).

———— 583 F 2nd 243 (1978).

Brown v. Board of Education of Topeka, 347 U.S. 483 (1954).

Brown II, 349 U.S. 294 (1955).

Callahan, R. E. (1962). *Education and the cult of efficiency.* Chicago, IL: The University of Chicago Press.

Carter, R. L. (1995). The unending struggle for equal educational opportunity. *Teachers College Record, 96*(4), 619–626.

Cincinnati Bureau of Governmental Research, Inc. (1953). *A study of 8 local school districts.* Cincinnati, OH: Author.

Cincinnati City Planning Commission. (1925). *The official city plan of Cincinnati, Ohio.* Cincinnati, OH: Author.

———— (1948). *The Cincinnati metropolitan master plan and the official city plan of the city of Cincinnati.* Cincinnati, OH: Author.

City problems of Lincoln Heights lead to similar woes for schools. (1970, June 17). *The Cincinnati Enquirer,* p. 10.

Community gives up destiny over schools. (1970, June 14). *The Cincinnati Enquirer,* p. 7A.

County, Lockland, Princeton, Wyoming to plan education for Lincoln Heights pupils: State board of education revokes district charter. (1969, December 11). *The Mill Creek Valley News,* p. 1.

Cranor, J. D., Crawley, G. L., & Scheele, R. H. (1989). Educational inequalities and opportunity in economic perspective. *American Journal of Political Science, 33*(1), 222–239.

Dabney, W. P. (1926). *Cincinnati's colored citizens.* Cincinnati, OH: Dabney Publishing.

Darling-Hammond, L. (2000). New standards and old inequalities: School reform and the education of African American students. *Journal of Negro Education, 69*(4), 263–87.

Delgado, R. (Ed.) (1995). *Critical race theory: The cutting edge.* Philadelphia, PA: Temple University Press.

DuBois, W. E. B. (1903). The talented tenth. In A. G. Paschal (Ed.), *A W. E. B. DuBois reader* (pp. 31–51). New York, NY: Macmillan.

Fletcher, R. S. (1943). *A history of Oberlin College: From its foundation through the Civil War.* Oberlin, OH: Oberlin College.

Former Wright plant is part of rich area. (1950/1979). *The Cincinnati Independent.* Reprinted in *The Lincoln Heights Journal, 1*(2), 1.

Giglierano, G. J., & Overmyer, D. A. (1988). *The bicentennial guide to Greater Cincinnati: A portrait of two hundred years.* Cincinnati, OH: The Cincinnati Historical Society.

Hamilton County Board of Education (1950, October 16). Resume of the state plan for consolidation of the Hamilton County school districts. The Princeton Museum of Education, second floor reading room, consolidation file drawer, 515 Greenwood Avenue, Cincinnati, Ohio 45246.

Hamilton County Board of Education meeting minutes (1951, March 13). The Princeton Museum of Education, second floor reading room, county minutes file drawer, 515 Greenwood Avenue, Cincinnati, Ohio 45246.

Harris, C. (1995). Whiteness as property. In K. Crenshaw, N. Gotanda, G. Peller, & K. Thomas (Eds.), *Critical race theory: The key writings that formed the movement.* (pp. 276–291). New York, NY: The New Press.

Harris, G. I., & Erickson, R. B. (1951). *A study of consolidation and redistricting in Hamilton County schools.* Cincinnati, OH: Hamilton County Research Foundation.

Harris, G. I., & Erickson, R. B. (1952). *A story of consolidation.* Cincinnati, OH: Hamilton County Research Foundation.

Jacobs, G. S. (1998). *Getting around Brown: Desegregation, development, and the Columbus public schools.* Columbus, OH: Ohio State University Press.

Keyes v. Denver School District No. 1, 413 U.S. 189 (1973).

Kluger, R. (1977). *Simple justice: The history of Brown v. Board of Education and Black America's struggle for equality.* New York, NY: Vintage Books.

Ladson-Billings, G., & Tate, W. (1995). Toward a critical race theory of education. *Teachers College Record, 97*(1), 47–68.

Lawrence, C. R. (1995). The id, the ego, and equal protection: reckoning with unconscious racism. In K. Crenshaw, N. Gotanda, G. Peller, & K. Thomas (Eds.), *Critical race theory: The key writings that formed the movement.* (pp. 235–257). New York, NY: The New Press.

Leigh, P. R. (1997). Segregation by gerrymander: The creation of the Lincoln Heights (Ohio) School District. *Journal of Negro Education, 66* (2), 121–136.

Lincoln Heights Board of Education meeting minutes (1951, February 7). The Princeton Museum of Education, second floor reading room, Lincoln Heights shelf, 515 Greenwood Avenue, Cincinnati, Ohio 45246.

———— (1968, February 8). The Princeton Museum of Education, second floor reading room, Lincoln Heights shelf, 515 Greenwood Avenue, Cincinnati, Ohio 45246.

———— (1968, July 11). The Princeton Museum of Education, second floor reading room, Lincoln Heights shelf, 515 Greenwood Avenue, Cincinnati, Ohio 45246.

———— (1969, July 12). The Princeton Museum of Education, second floor reading room, Lincoln Heights shelf, 515 Greenwood Avenue, Cincinnati, Ohio 45246.

———— (1969, December 2). The Princeton Museum of Education, second floor reading room, Lincoln Heights shelf, 515 Greenwood Avenue, Cincinnati, Ohio 45246.

Lincoln Heights grows since incorporation in '46. (1970, June 16). *The Cincinnati_Enquirer*, p. 13.

Lincoln Heights: Now a chance to overcome most difficulties of the past. (1974, September 16). *The Cincinnati Enquirer*, p. 19.

Lincoln Heights seeks to join Princeton School District. (1970, January 15). *The Cincinnati Post & Times-Star*, p. 11.

Lucas, R. E. (1971). Princeton's investment in children provides new opportunities for all. *Mini Journal 4*(1), 2–8.

———— (1976). Lincoln Heights–Princeton merger—five years later. *Mini Journal, 7*(2), 2–9.

Luke, M. (1981a, March). Twenty-five years of progress at Princeton. *Princeton Piper, 17*(2), 5.

———— (1981b, July). Princeton history: Excitement, challenge. *Princeton Piper, 17*(3), 5–8.

———— (1982, February). Princeton history: Excitement and progress. *Princeton Piper, 18*(1), 3–8.

Miami University, Bureau of Educational Field Services. (1961). *Lincoln Heights: Its people, its schools, its future.* Oxford, OH: Author.

Miller, Z. L. (1981). *Suburb: Neighborhood and community in Forest Park, Ohio, 1935–1976.* Knoxville, TN: The University of Tennessee Press.

No "demands" have been made of Princeton. (1970, January 22). *Mill Creek Valley News*, p. 1.

Orfield, G., Eaton, S. E., & The Harvard Project on School Desegregation. (1996). *Dismantling desegregation: The quiet reversal of Brown v. Board of Education.* New York, NY: The New Press.

Penick v. Columbus Board of Education, 429 F. Supp. 229.

Reed, D. D., & Reed, T. H. (1953). *The Cincinnati area must solve its metropolitan problems.* Cincinnati, OH: Dunie Printing Co.

Robinson W. (1969, December 9). School units to plan Lincoln Heights fate. *The Cincinnati Post & Times-Star*, p. 12.

———— (1970a, January 15). Lincoln Hgts. is fighting for a chance. *The Cincinnati Post & Times-Star*, p. 1.

———— (1970b, March 3). Lincoln Heights merger protest is orderly at Princeton school. *The Cincinnati Post & Times-Star*, p. 7.

Roget, P. M. (1994). *Roget's thesaurus of English words and phrases.* Seattle, WA: Microsoft Corporation.

Russo, C. J., Harris, J., & Sandidge, R. F. (1994). *Brown v. Board of Education* at 40: A legal history of equal educational opportunities in American public education. *Journal of Negro Education, 63*(3), 297–309.

Schools big hurdle in annexation path. (1951, October 28). *The Cincinnati Enquirer*, p. 37.

Segregation in Lincoln Heights topic of Columbus meetings. (1969, August 14). *The Cincinnati Post & Times-Star*, p. 34.

Simms, G. (1970, March 19). Merger has plus, minus: Lincoln Heights feelings mixed. *The Cincinnati Post & Times-Star*, p. 15.

Small tax base and no space to expand hurt Lincoln Heights. (1970, June 18). *The Cincinnati Enquirer*, p. 25.

Solorzano, D., Cela, M., & Yosso, T. (2000). Critical race theory, racial microaggressions, and campus racial climate: The experiences of African American college students. *Journal of Negro Education, 69* (1–2), 60–73.

State and local leaders meet to determine how Lincoln Heights children to be educated. (1969, October 2). *The Mill Creek Valley News*, p. 2.

Sundstrom, W. A. (1994). The color line: Racial norms and discrimination in urban labor markets, 1910–1950. *Journal of Economic History, 54*(2), 382–396.

Swann v. Charlotte-Mecklenberg Board of Education, 402 U.S. 1 (1971).

Synnott, M. G. (1979). *The half opened door: Discrimination and admissions at Harvard, Yale, and Princeton, 1900–1970.* Westport, CT: Greenwood Press.

Tate, W. (1996). Critical race theory and education: History, theory, and implications. *Review of Research in Education, 22* 195–247.

Taylor, H. L. (1979). *The building of a black industrial suburb: The Lincoln Heights, Ohio story.* Doctoral dissertation, University of New York, Buffalo.

———— (1984). The use of maps in the study of the Black ghetto-formation process. *Historical Methods 17*(2), 44–58.

———— (1993). City building, public policy, the rise of the industrial city and Black ghetto–slum formation in Cincinnati, 1850–1940. In H. L. Taylor (Ed.), *Race and the city* (pp. 156–208). Urbana, IL: University of Illinois Press.

"Too little"—that's story of Lincoln Heights. (1970, June 15). *The Cincinnati Enquirer*, p. 11.

Urban, W., & Wagoner, J. (1996). *American education: A history.* New York: McGraw-Hill.

U.S. Department of Commerce, Bureau of the Census. (1940). *Sixteenth census of the United States, 1940: Population and housing.* Washington, DC: U.S. Government Printing Office.

———— (1950). *Seventeenth census of the United States, 1950: Population and housing.* Washington, DC: Government Printing Office.

Washington, B. T. (1901). *Up From slavery: An autobiography.* Garden City, NY: Doubleday.

Watras, J. (1997). *Politics, race, and schools: Racial integration, 1954–1994.* New York, NY: Garland Publishing, Inc.

Webber, T. L. (1978). *Deep like the rivers: Education in the slave quarter community, 1831–1865.* New York, NY: W. W. Norton.

Weiss, A. (1995). Human capital vs. signalling explanations of wages. *Journal of Economic Perspectives, 9*(4), 133–154.

Wheat, W. (1969, December 9). State Revokes Charter of Lincoln Hgts. school. *The Cincinnati Enquirer*, p. 20.

——— (1970, February 4). "Orphan" students to Princeton. *The Cincinnati Enquirer*, p. 1.

Wheeler, L. (1996, March). They call it education. *Ohio Magazine, 18*(10), pp. 15–17,19.